g-C
RSTO

The American Exploration and Travel Series

(COMPLETE LIST ON PAGE 180)

THE PLAINS

The Plains

Being No Less Than a Collection
of Veracious Memoranda
Taken During the Expedition of Exploration
in the year 1845, From the western settlements
of Missouri to the Mexican Border,
and from Bent's Fort on the Arkansas to Fort Gibson,
via South Fork of Canadian—North Mexico and
North-western Texas

by
François des Montaignes

EDITED AND WITH AN INTRODUCTION

BY

NANCY ALPERT MOWER

AND

DON RUSSELL

Norman
University of Oklahoma Press

International Standard Book Number: 0–8061–0998–X

Library of Congress Catalog Card Number: 70–177341

Copyright 1972 by the University of Oklahoma Press, Publishing Division of the University. Composed and printed at Norman, Oklahoma, U.S.A., by the University of Oklahoma Press. First edition.

The Plains is Volume 60 in *The American Exploration and Travel Series.*

ACKNOWLEDGMENT

I wish to thank Scripps College for permission to publish this journal. Special thanks go to Joseph Arnold Foster, Professor of English Emeritus of Scripps, who first stimulated my interest in Western literature, and who so carefully guided and aided me in my original analysis of *The Plains* as a baccalaureate thesis. I express sincere appreciation to French R. Fogle and the late Robert Glass Cleland for suggesting and encouraging this edition of Montaignes' journal and to the staffs of the Henry E. Huntington Memorial Library, San Marino, California; the Honnold Library, Claremont, California; and the Library of Congress, Washington, D.C., for invaluable aid in research.

NANCY ALPERT MOWER

CONTENTS

ILLUSTRATIONS

The illustrations for this edition were taken from Montaignes' original journal. Courtesy Ella Strong Denison Library, Scripps College, Claremont, California.

MAP

EDITORS' INTRODUCTION

In the middle decades of the nineteenth century, John Charles Frémont, "The Pathfinder," was a national hero. Yet every step of his career was marked by controversy. To this day there is sharp disagreement about his worth and accomplishment. Those who have studied his career closely are wary of claiming too much for him. "Again and again promised triumph turned into sorry futility," Allan Nevins points out. Though impulsive and a poor judge of men, Frémont had "extreme quickness of mind and some very brilliant qualities."[1] Another biographer remarks, "Morally Frémont was a loose constructionist. He adjusted his moral outlook very largely to the environment in which he lived." Nevertheless, his "entire career was built largely on a series of circumstances over which he exercised little or no control."[2]

Frémont was illegitimate—a heavy strike against him in nineteenth-century America. His mother eloped from a husband nearly fifty years her senior to lead a vagabond existence. John Charles was born on January 21, 1813, in Savannah, according to most authorities, although an army record makes it South Carolina. As a young man in Charleston, he won the backing of a patron who sent him to preparatory school where he made a brilliant record, but he later left Charleston College without completing a degree.

Frémont won the favor of one of South Carolina's most eminent citizens, Joel Roberts Poinsett, immortalized because as minister to Mexico he brought back the red Christmas flower that bears his name. As secretary of war under President Van Buren, Poinsett appointed Frémont a second lieutenant in the Corps of Topo-

---

[1] Allan Nevins, *Frémont, Pathmarker of the West,* 618–19.
[2] Cardinal Goodwin, *John Charles Frémont: An Explanation of His Career,* 260.

graphical Engineers, a separate branch of army service from the Corps of Engineers, consisting entirely of officers charged with making maps, plans, surveys, and explorations. It was headed by Colonel John James Abert, a stern soldier and shrewd politician.

In Washington, Frémont courted Jessie Benton, whose father, the influential Senator Thomas Hart Benton of Missouri, was a strong advocate of manifest destiny and westward expansion. Despite early opposition to his prospective son-in-law, heightened by a runaway marriage, Senator Benton was won over, backing Frémont with all his prestige until the Pathfinder became Republican candidate for the presidency in 1856.

Much secrecy surrounded the first Frémont expedition in 1842. The route followed the Oregon Trail, which was in no particular need of exploration at that date, but Senator Benton, who maneuvered the expedition's modest appropriation through Congress, had some idea of meddling in Oregon, a territory still held jointly with Great Britain. To what extent Colonel Abert, who issued the orders—and modified them at Frémont's request to include South Pass—knew of Benton's machinations is not clear. Almost certainly, President John Tyler and Secretary of War John C. Spencer were kept in the dark. Thus Frémont learned the bad habit of ignoring higher authority that was to bring him to grief eventually. Happily, no opportunity for twisting the lion's tail occurred. The expedition proved a great success in exploration, but perhaps its triumph came in the official report Frémont filed. Encouraged and possibly abetted by Jessie, he produced a congressional document that was adventure story, travel book, and emigrants' guide. As occasionally happens even in our own time, a government publication became a best seller.

A second expedition, with objectives similar to the first, followed in 1843–44. The announced purpose was to connect the reconnaissance of 1842 with the surveys of Commander Charles Wilkes on the coast of the Pacific Ocean, but again there was secrecy. As part of his equipment, Frémont made requisition for a twelve-pound howitzer. When Colonel Abert learned of this, he ordered Frémont to return to Washington to explain why he needed artillery on a scientific expedition. Jessie intercepted the message and sent her husband on his way, cannon and all, before he knew of the order. Senator Benton took responsibility for his daughter's action and condemned the reprimand implied in Abert's instructions.

In reply, Colonel Abert said of the howitzer: "Now as the equipment of his party contemplated a serious change in the character of the expedition under his command, one that might involve the Government in Indian hostility, I have no doubt you will admit it to have been a negligence deserving some reproach that he did not seek the advice and orders of the Department. The Department might, under such anticipations, have prohibited the expedition, or it might have made it adequate successfully to have encountered the contemplated emergency."[3]

Abert probably knew as well as Benton that Indian hostility was not the contemplated emergency, but having put the Senator in his place for once, he let the matter drop and held no grudges. Abert had nursed the Topographical Engineers to corps status, but the Frémont-Benton team was giving it publicity and appropriations. The Colonel could afford to overlook idiosyncrasies in his subordinate and ignore the expansionist machinations of the Senate leader. Despite the clash, Abert seems to have taken considerable pride in Frémont's accomplishments.

Frémont's expedition traversed Oregon to Fort Vancouver without antagonizing the British. He then turned south, abandoned his howitzer in the snows of the Sierras, and visited California without becoming entangled with Mexican authorities. Again there was an official report, an even more successful ad-

---

[3] William H. Goetzmann, *Army Exploration in the American West, 1803-1863*, 66–67. Nevins, *Frémont*, 133, missed Abert's reply.

venture story, with a hero—Kit Carson—who might well have come out of a dime novel and of course eventually did. But this was not all. Because Frémont was well educated in the sciences of his day, says William H. Goetzmann, "the spirit of contemporary science was present in every page of his final report." Goetzmann concludes that "his contributions derived from three aspects of his type of exploration: Its comprehensiveness, its manner of presentation, and the relative trustworthiness of the authority upon which it rested."[4]

Frémont reached the height of his fame as an explorer with the second expedition. Dispute and controversy marked almost every step of the third expedition in 1845–46. In its planning, Frémont emphasized scientific aspects, and he did accomplish something with his survey of the Great Basin. To many, including the journalist with whom we are concerned here, the third expedition seemed clearly a filibustering party recruited to seize California if opportunity offered. That, of course, is what happened. The expedition reached California in December, 1845. Mexican officials, suspicious of its scientific character, ordered it to leave. After some defiant bluster, Frémont started toward Oregon but was overtaken by Marine Corps Lieutenant Archibald F. Gillespie with a message the substance of which has never been revealed. In any event, Frémont turned back, supported the Bear Flag revolt, and, after it became known that there was war with Mexico, co-operated with Commodore Robert F. Stockton in taking California.

When Brigadier General Stephen Watts Kearny arrived in California, Frémont declined to accept his authority. Tried by court-martial for mutiny and disobedience to orders, Frémont was found guilty and sentenced to dismissal from the army. President James K. Polk approved the verdict, except in regard

---

[4] Goetzmann, *Army Exploration*, 103–104.

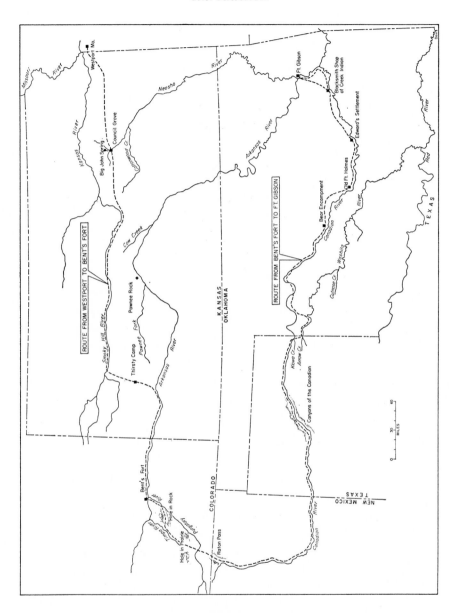

ROUTE OF THE EXPEDITION, 1845

to mutiny, and remitted the sentence. This did not satisfy Frémont, who resigned immediately.[5]

If this survey seems too critical of Frémont, it is because of the attempt to emphasize aspects of his career that have a bearing on the journal with which we are concerned. The war with Mexico was one of our least popular wars, and much that concerns it is still obscured by emotion and hasty judgment. There is no point in debating Frémont's part in it, but as a result of his resignation, no official report of his third expedition ever appeared. A "thorough and complete report" was still being promised in 1856, when Frémont was a candidate for President.[6] The result, apparently, was Frémont's *Memoirs of My Life*, not published until 1886 and containing little about the first stage of the expedition.

Isaac Cooper, who used the nom de plume François des Montaignes in writing his "veracious memoranda"—there seems no question about the identification—joined the Frémont expedition at St. Louis and accompanied its members on the steamboat *Henry Bry* to Westport and on foot to a camp on Boone's Fork where the company organized.

The Frémont Third Expedition started west on June 23, 1845. The caravan followed the Santa Fe Trail for three hundred miles to Pawnee Fork, a branch of the Arkansas River, traveled along the fork for a few days, then turned north, and crossed to the Smoky Hill Fork of the Kansas River. The party left the Smoky Hill Fork on July 29, turned south, and returned to the Santa Fe Trail along the Arkansas, arriving at Bent's Fort on August 1.

On August 10, Frémont detached thirty-five men as the "South Company," under command of Lieutenant James William Abert, with orders "to make a survey of the Canadian, from its source

---

[5] Dwight L. Clarke, *Stephen Watts Kearny, Soldier of the West*, 347–73, contains a detailed account of the court-martial, correcting some extravagant statements made in Frémont's behalf.

[6] Charles Wentworth Upham, *Life, Explorations, and Public Services of John Charles Fremont*, 209.

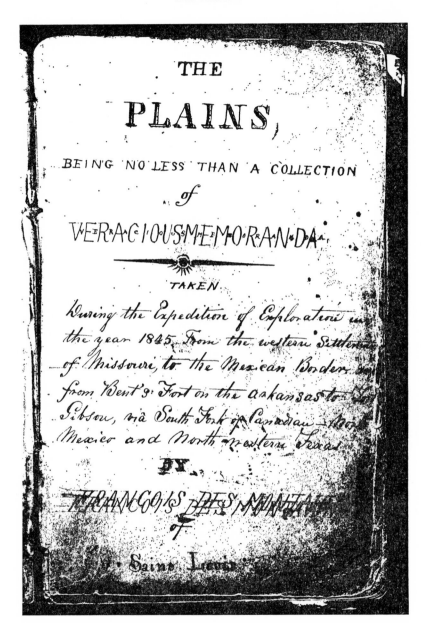

THE
PLAINS,
BEING NO LESS THAN A COLLECTION
of
VERACIOUSMEMORANDA.
TAKEN
During the Expedition of Exploration in
the year 1845, from the western Settlements
of Missouri, to the Mexican Border, and
from Bent's Fort on the Arkansas to Fort
Gibson, via South Fork of Canadian.—North
Mexico and North-western Texas.
BY
FRANCOIS DES MONTAIGNES
of
Saint Louis

TITLE PAGE OF MONTAIGNES' JOURNAL

to its junction with the Arkansas, taking in on the way the Purgatory River and the Head Waters of the Washita, called by the
Indians Buffalo Creek and Cut-Nose Creek."[7] Cooper, alias
Montaignes, was assigned to the South Company. Thus his journal
covers only the first and least important part of the Frémont
expedition, describing what was by that time a common route of
travel. It is, however, the only detailed account of this leg of
the expedition, and it throws much light on the company's organization and motives. Lieutenant Abert made an official report of
his reconnaissance, to which the Montaignes journal is a useful
supplement written from the point of view of a hired hand.

Montaignes records that Frémont "declared his intention to
have no journals kept in his camp," saying, "I'll do my own
writing." This secrecy may have relation to the cloak-and-dagger
character of the expedition, but it leaves the impression that the
Captain sought to eliminate rivals in its literary aspects. Undoubt-
edly this prohibition accounts for Cooper's adopting a pseudonym. That Cooper did keep a journal seems evident, although
the version we have is an expanded manuscript prepared for
publication or as a permanent record.

It is written in a leather-bound notebook, 3¾ by 5¾ inches
in size, which seems to have consisted originally of 220 pages, 24
of which are now missing. The writing is in ink with some pencil
notations. The manuscript was prepared in imitation of a printed
book, with titles and summaries at the head of each chapter and
occasional quotations in verse, in the custom of the time. There
are a few footnotes. Two styles of handwriting are used: an
upright, vertical hand for chapter titles and summaries, and a
somewhat smaller, sloped hand for the text. Eight drawings and
some ornamentation supplement the text.

Cooper's title-page follows: The / Plains / Being No Less Than
a Collection / of / Veracious Memoranda / (ornament) / taken

[7] *Journal of Lieutenant J. W. Abert from Bent's Fort to St. Louis in 1845*, 8.

During the Expedition of Exploration in / the year 1845. From the western settlements / of Missouri, to the Mexican Border, and / from Bent's Fort on the Arkansas to Fort / Gibson, via South Fork of Canadian—North / Mexico and North-western Texas. / by / Francois des Montaignes / of / Saint Louis / 1846.

This date seems to indicate that the manuscript was prepared in 1846—except that opposite the title page is pasted an unidentified clipping reviewing the September, 1853, number of *The Western Journal and Civilian,* in which was printed "the eleventh chapter of a series by *Francois des Montaignes,* descriptive of life on the plains. Francois was a member of the Frémont exploring expedition of 1845, and is now arranging his elaborate collection of memoranda in shape for preservation." This would argue that we have a manuscript arranged after magazine serialization. Before leaving the anonymous reviewer, we might add his comment: "The tone of the sketches is light and occasionally humorous. We have ever found them entertaining."

The serialization in *The Western Journal and Civilian,* a monthly magazine printed in St. Louis, began in the issue of October, 1852 (Volume IX, Number 1), and continued monthly through the five remaining numbers of that volume and the six numbers of Volume X to September, 1853. That this came to eleven chapters is explained by the installment of January, 1853, scheduled as continuing Chapter III from the December issue. Chapter XII appeared two and one-half years after Chapter XI—in the issue of March, 1856 (Volume XV, Number 4). No explanation was offered for the long delay other than the legend, "Continued from page 445, Vol. 10, Western Journal."

That was all, although the twelve chapters printed in thirteen installments, some of them quite short, include only five of the eighteen manuscript chapters, not quite covering the story of the Frémont expedition as far as Bent's Fort. There are other discrepancies, including the interpolation of new material, which in one case amounts to three installments of the printed text. Added factual material is rare, however. Much of the change is in euphuistic verbiage and extraneous observation.

Whether the author was responsible for both versions or whether the magazine editor enlivened the narrative to make it more presentable to his readers are questions that cannot be answered from the data available to us. It was a period when fine writing was esteemed; when the written word was expected to be more than a mere presentation of facts; when figures, flowers, and literary and classical allusions distinguished the professional writer from the amateur. Compare, for example, Washington Irving's *A Tour of the Prairies* with the original material on which it is based, published as *The Western Journals of Washington Irving.*[8] Some modern readers may prefer the original journals, but in either case, neither Isaac Cooper, alias François des Montaignes, nor his editor was a Washington Irving.

The manuscript is less elegant and stays a little closer to the facts than the serialization. Occasionally a name appears that is omitted in the original. Many of those who accompanied the expedition are more important to the historian than they were to their contemporaries—"Broken Hand" Fitzpatrick, John Hatcher, and François La Tulippe, for example. Montaignes may make a real contribution in his tales in the Mountain Man's dialect, of which we have few contemporary examples. Here also his humor is at its best. Some of his attempts to be funny do not quite succeed, although the crude practical jokes he describes are typical of the period. Like the anonymous contemporary reviewer, "We have ever found him entertaining."

Montaignes' sharp criticism of Frémont will disturb many who regard the Pathfinder as a peerless hero and adventurer. More aspersions appear in the manuscript than in the printed version, although in at least one case derogatory comment is amplified

[8] *The Western Journals of Washington Irving* (ed. by John Francis McDermott).

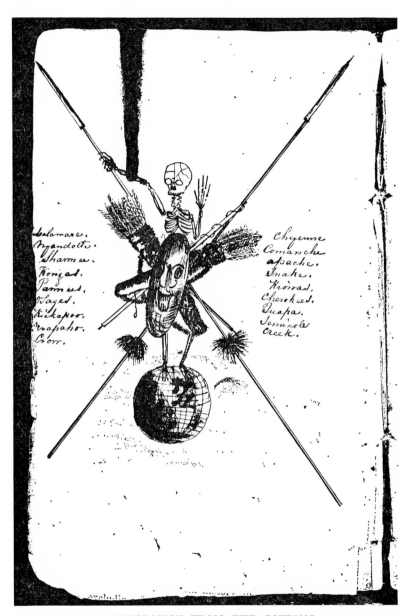

A DECORATION FROM THE JOURNAL

in the *Western Journal*. This refers to the speech in which Frémont declared martial law and banned the keeping of journals, prompting ten or eleven men to quit the expedition.

Frémont's unpopularity with those who accompanied him is shown in the recent discovery and translation of the diaries of Charles Preuss, cartographer on the first, second, and fourth expeditions. Apparently Frémont made a habit of forbidding journals, since Preuss, too, kept his diaries secret. Preuss tells of a quarrel with Kit Carson: "Frémont got excited, as usual . . . developed a headache." Again, "Frémont began to rave again, wanted to dismiss everybody, go home immediately, etc. etc." Eventually Frémont calmed down, but, says Preuss, "This and other small troubles and annoyances had gotten on Frémont's nerves, which is not surprising with a childishly passionate man like him."[9]

Objections to Frémont's disciplinary methods may be taken with a grain of salt. Discipline in unmilitary expeditions was a problem, and Frémont should not be condemned for displaying something less than the best possible leadership. An incident occurring at Dry Creek on July 30, 1845, is less forgivable. The night before, members of one mess had had the foresight to fill a keg with water and place it in their wagon. The next night, as they lighted their fires to prepare coffee, Frémont's servant appeared and demanded the water. Says Montaignes: "The fire burnt splendid at the tent of the Captain and fragrant odours as of boiling coffee greeted the nasal organs of the thirsty camp, proceeding from the coffeepot for the Captain's own use."

This bit of arrogance goes far toward justifying Montaignes' accusations that Frémont's larder was always full of luxuries denied his men and that he was indifferent to laying in a supply of meat when buffalo were first found in numbers.

The weight to be given Montaignes' strictures depends to some

[9] Charles Preuss, *Exploring with Frémont*, 40, 46.

degree on what we know of the author, and that unfortunately is very little. There is a fragment—literally—of a hint explaining his joining the expedition.

It has been mentioned that some pages of the notebook are missing, torn out, as remaining stubs attest. What appears to be the last page of a discarded introduction reads:

> . . . proceeds to California."
>
> "Yes Sir" replied the young man, "I was already informed of that. But if I now start for California with you, I do not wish to leave the Company untill I arrive there."
>
> "Oh no! Certainly not!"
>
> "And when I get there, if I like the Country I suppose I can have it at my will to remain, and if I do not like it, I can remain with your Company untill its return."
>
> "Oh yes! to be Sure: I have no objections to that" replied the Captain, "But I wish our agreement to be secret as you are the only one with whom I have made such a one. Therefore have all your arrangements made by evening, as there will be a boat starting for Kanzas with a party of our men."
>
> "Aye, Aye, Sir!" and the youth retired to make his arrangements.

The dialogue is evidently between François des Montaignes and Captain Frémont. It indicates that their relations were pleasant at the start. It indicates also that the expedition was going to California, although we know that Frémont's orders did not so specify. That may have been one of the reasons behind his request for secrecy. Clearly, Montaignes intended to go to California with Frémont. The journal does not explain why he did not. Quite possibly Frémont took the occasion to rid himself of a malcontent by assigning Montaignes to Abert's company. It is evident that Montaignes was quite happy to be free of Frémont's command.

The missing pages of the introduction might throw some light on Montaignes' reasons for joining the expedition. What kind of man would undertake such a journey? He was to be away from home and family, if he had either, for some six months. Had he gone on to California, he might not have returned for years. Fifteen miles or so a day muleback, horseback, or afoot was promised, through prairie, desert, or mountains, in alternating intense heat and uncomfortable cold. Many nights would be spent in watersoaked tents and blankets. There was no guarantee of food except what could be supplied by hunters. The party would enter country infested with Indians whose dispositions toward intruders were unknown—Cheyennes, Kansas, Arapahos, Comanches, Kiowas, Apaches, Pawnees. Gold had not yet been discovered in California, so there was no promise of sudden wealth, certainly not from the wages paid Frémont's hired hands. What sort of man would be attracted by such prospects—loafer, vagabond, ne'er-do-well, or just youthful adventurer?

Nearly all that can be learned of Montaignes is drawn from internal evidence. Of being thrown by a mule, he says, "Such was the youth's first debut on the stage of prairie life." He refers continually to the "young greenhorns" of the expedition, implying that he is one of them. He finds it a new experience to know voyageurs and Mountain Men, and he is able to tell us something about them from a fresh point of view. His straining for humor and fine writing may be annoying, but he usually desists before reaching the point of absurdity. On the whole, François makes a good impression upon his reader. We part friends, wishing we could know a bit more about him.

Identification of François des Montaignes as Isaac Cooper rests on the following evidence. Moye Stephens, who owned the original manuscript of the diary, "informed us that François' real name was Isaac Cooper," says Henry R. Wagner's *The Plains and the Rockies*. The name Isaac Cooper appears at the top of Lieutenant Abert's list of men comprising the expedition from Bent's Fort to St. Louis. One of the clippings attached to the inside front cover of the diary notebook refers to a Mr. I. J. Cooper as "a literateur of rare freshness and vivacity." In the journal, the author makes one apparently unintentional slip in referring to himself as Cooper but includes a purposeful poetic apologia indicating that François des Montaignes was a pseudonym.

Wagner adds that Cooper "was from Missouri and his wife's sister married B. D. Wilson, the California pioneer." Isaac Cooper seems to have spent his later years in Alhambra, California, where he died, leaving two sons, Ike and Tom. One of these, probably Ike, was the first ranger in Los Angeles National Forest. He gave the journal to Moye Stephens. It passed from Stephens to his brother-in-law, Dr. Frick of Claremont, California, who presented it to Scripps College in 1953. The manuscript is now in the Ella Strong Denison Library, Scripps College, Claremont, California.

A word on the text is perhaps in order. The endeavor has been to present the journal in its original form as nearly as possible, including spelling and punctuation, even when the author himself has been inconsistent. His capitalization has not been maintained throughout, because it is not always clear what form of certain letters he intends as capitals. Occasional changes in capitalization and punctuation are made to clarify his apparent intent. Unintentional repetitions of words have been deleted. Montaignes' original footnotes are retained.

THE PLAINS

Caravan of Explorers. *"En Route."*

CHAPTER ONE

Which kills two birds with one stone, as it introduces the youth François des Montaignes to some fellow-voyagers, and the Steamer Henry Bry *to Kanzas on the Missouri River.*

$\mathbb{B}$E it known to all good readers, that, during the 3rd, 4th, & 5th days of June 1845,—the good steamer, *Henry Bry*, Chouteau master,[1] had been threatening and promising to start for Missouri River every hour, yet the 6th came and she had but just left the port of Saint Louis. On this craft, there were some twenty-odd souls, who, from their independent swagger and jovial carriage, appeared to belong to some party about to start for Oregon or California. They were mostly young Americans healthy and full of fun and elasticity, yet there were some 4 or 5 others aboard the vessel, who preserved a more serious exterior and now and then gave utterance to some pithy ejaculation of contempt at the sayings and doings of the set of greenhorns, who they felt confident of being their inferiors in the coming profession of mountain travelling. These spoke that mongrel language, so extensively in use among the Creoles of the West and which although a piebald patois of the French, is much better known by the appellation of Canadian. These men were Canadian—men, experienced in the manner and modes of exploring wild mountainous regions—of threading desert plains—of killing the wild beasts of these regions—of trading with and of conciliating the barbarous inhabitants thereof—of packing ani-

1 Possibly Charles Pierre Chouteau, son of Pierre Chouteau, Jr., who, returning to St. Louis from the London office in 1845, took a personal interest in the fur company's navigation problems. John E. Sunder, *The Fur Trade on the Upper Missouri, 1840–1865*, 131.

mals—of every thing in fact which is necessary to be done during an expedition through wild and savage Indians and through untrodden regions. Several had already been engagés in previous trips of the kind—whilst every one of them had been engaged, at least a year or two, at some trading post of the American Fur Company.[2] Therefore, when such men as these, who, experienced in every thing of the kind, were well aware of what was yet to come, cast a dubious and almost sneering look at the too-playful and sanguine group of verdant ones on board, it should have tamed their fun toute-de-suite—and ought by all means to have terrified some of the rascals into seriousness. But they, sorry devils, as they were, would not so much as cast a glance at the vieux voyageurs, much less keep their company.

To speak plainly, the present cargo of the *Henry Bry*, was by no means a choir of psalm-singers nor quakers. They eat, drank, talked, sang,—played cards and smoked cigars when they pleased and as much as they pleased. When the boat stopped at a wood yard, every son of them must needs go ashore and shoot at a spot. When they had no balls—they must go ashore any how to jump and run foot races,—and when they did not feel in the humour of jumping or racing, they must go ashore, by all means, for the sake only of being ashore. This conduct on the part of the American engagés might perhaps have pleased the Captain,[3] who was

---

[2] "American Fur Company" at this time meant Pierre Chouteau, Jr., and Company, which in 1843 took over the upper Mississippi fur trade from Ramsey Crooks—who also continued to use the name "American Fur Company." *Ibid.*, 15–16. The company, incorporated in New York by John Jacob Astor in 1809, had many affiliates and subsidiaries. In 1834, Astor sold its "Northern Department" to Crooks. Paul Chrisler Phillips and J. W. Smurr, *The Fur Trade.*

[3] "The Captain" always refers to John Charles Frémont, leader of the expedition. In lineal rank he was still a second lieutenant in the Corps of Topographical Engineers. On July 31, 1844, at the instance of Major General Winfield Scott, Frémont received the double brevet of first lieutenant and captain "for gallant and highly meritorious service in two expeditions to the Rocky Mountains" terminating October 17, 1842, and July 31, 1844. In this period, staff departments were manned largely with officers serving in brevet ranks, so Frémont would be assigned to duty in his brevet rank (with pay as captain) for the third expedition.

on board with us,—but no doubt he frequently shook his head, and muttered to himself "These chaps are green and nimble enough now, but by the time they are a month's travel on the prairie, I'll lay a wager, there be not much desire to run foot races."

There were also on board the *Henry Bry*, besides the Captain and hands, several officers—lieutenants of the army, gay young fellows, who were about to accompany the expedition, apparently more for the purpose of killing dull time than any thing else.[4]

The voyage from St Louis to Kanzas was soon made; for the days slipped by most pleasantly to all hands—occupied in the manner I have stated in doing everything but anything.

Finally after passing numerous towns and pseudo-cities in embryo which spotted the banks of the Missouri on each side,— on the morning of the 9th—being Monday, the little port of Kanzas—the Westport landing came in sight[5]—and now was all hurry and confusion.

Each man grasped his possible sack, which by the way is a provincial name for clothes sack, in one hand and his blankets and rifle in the other, and stood ready to leap ashore.

As the boat touched the shore, there ensued no tremendous

[4] The lieutenants were James William Abert of New Jersey and William Guy Peck of Connecticut, both brevet second lieutenants of the Corps of Topographical Engineers. Abert was graduated from West Point in 1842 and served for one year in the 5th Infantry before being transferred to the Topographical Engineers. The brevet rank was given because there were no vacancies in Regular Army assignments. Abert did not become second lieutenant until 1846. The son of Colonel John James Abert, chief of the Corps of Topographical Engineers, he attained the ranks of major and brevet lieutenant colonel during the Civil War. He died on August 10, 1897. Peck was graduated from West Point in 1844 as brevet second lieutenant of Topographical Engineers and did not reach the full rank until 1848. He became first lieutenant in 1853, resigned in 1855, and died on February 7, 1892.

[5] Westport Landing was purchased by the Kansas Town Company in 1838. Eventually it became Kansas City, Missouri. John C. McCoy, who had platted Westport in 1833, built the landing the following year. The distance from the landing to Westport, four to six miles, depending on the route taken through the mud bottoms described by Montaignes, was much shorter than the eighteen or so miles to the landing at Independence, and Westport soon became the rendezvous point for wagon trains starting over the Santa Fe and Oregon trails.

rush of draymen—friends—relations—and porters, such as welcome the arrival of a Steamer in some great Port,—but there did
ensue a rush of Americans—Canadians—officers &c, to land.

It was raining in one of those dull moods in which a hazy
morning in Missouri is so frequently opened, and by the time
we had carried our guns and baggage to a place of security, the
wharf or landing was a complete mudhole.—The horses had
been taken out some 3 or 4 miles below us—and we next proceeded to take forth the barrels of flour—of sugar—of coffee—
the boxes of rice, of this & that—the bales of one thing and
another—the bundles of iron pickets—the long & short boxes of
rifles and of instruments—of this and that, and lastly several
hogsheads of bacon.

When at the end of Some 2 or 3 hours we found[6]

I wish not to weary the reader with too many trifling particulars
and shall therefore omit many things which might be included in
what is denominated a Journal. These however, which I shall
omit, have no relation with the main important subject and I
shall not consider anything as lost by their omission.

Suffice it therefore to say, that we and our share of the boat's
cargo was unshipped—The boat proceded on her way up the
river, and we endeavoured to make ourselves as comfortable as
circumstances would permit, by eating a hearty breakfast—taking a hearty dram and strolling through the little landing.

Waggons arrived from Westport about 11 o'clock to transport
the baggage and plunder to the camp which some said was near
Westport. But as we were all green, and did not happen to know
very well the situation of Westport and consequently of the camp
either, the conclusion was that none of us knew or could be
expected to know where the camp was.

However, as soon as the waggons were laden, we started out
one and all in parties of ten & 6 for the first camp near Westport.

6 This incomplete sentence is at the bottom of a manuscript page.

The first group was composed of ten or 12, wherof one among the rest was François des Montaignes, who, with his rifle on his shoulder, trudged along ahead of his companions with much sprightliness and gaité du coeur. Mile after mile was passed—the day was fast drawing to a close—and the voyagers now hoped soon to see the camp. Yet on they went,—the road had no end,—and they were fast becoming tired. A waggon[7] passed at a swift pace,—a few words passed—and when we arrived at Westport—a waggon stood waiting at the tavern door, to transport us to Boone's Fork 6 miles farther.[8]

Finally an hour by sun we reach the edge of that great plain or prairie which stretches out far & wide from the western boundary of Missouri to the feet of the Stony or Rocky Mountains and in its extent from North to South it has no confines. The rolls of the prairie before seemed heaved into beautifully rounding waves or surges by some great power, and when we reached the pinnacle of a lofty eminence and beheld the American camp on the prairie below us, it seemed like some distant fleet of vessels at anchor on a heaving sea.

Indeed we were all in an admirable condition to speculate on matters and things—for at the tavern of Westport all hands made a simultaneous rush at the bar and the whole crew one and all, by the time we left the town which we did with extraordinary éclat—yelling & shouting—were in a most pitiable condition of gloriousness, and adapted in every way to well appreciate the beauty of lanscapes and to poetize theron.

"Old Dan Tucker" that well patronized air and "Lucy Neal"

7 Both the manuscript and the printed version are inconsistent in spelling "waggons" with the doubled "g."

8 "Boone's Fork" seems to be so called only by Montaignes. Edward M. Kern, artist of the expedition, calls it "Camp, at the head of Boon Creek, Mo. Ter." Louise Barry, "Kansas Before 1854: A Revised Annals," Part Fourteen, *The Kansas Historical Quarterly*, Vol. XXX, No. 2 (Summer, 1964), 226. "Boone" may honor Daniel Morgan Boone, son of Daniel Boone, an early settler in the area, or his son Albert Gallatin Boone, who had a trading post in early Westport. "Boone's Fork," six miles west of Westport, was in Johnson County, Kansas.

were sung with rapture, and with a strain of most mournful music proceeding from our throats in the shape of some 5 or 6 different songs at once—our little waggon whirled into the Camp.

Our Captain was already here,—a couple of old and tempory tents were up and whilst several large rawboned fellows were cooking a meal,—the whole place was a crowd of hangers on or spectators, who as was supposed, had been lying in wait there for a week or more, in order to make arrangements with Capt Frémont to accompany his expedition.

The herds of mules & horses which belonged to the Expedition were feeding in the distance,[9] whilst every now and then a figure on horseback would flit across the darkening horizon, marking the presence of the horse guards.

The drove of animals were driven up to the camp at dark, & confined in an enclosure made by felling trees in such a manner as by their fall to form a circle—called in Spanish a "Caral."[10] Such was the appearance of the camp when our advanced group took possession of it.

The first night of our sojourn at this camp on the prairie was rather inauspicious,—for the clouds grew black as ebony and the thunder rolled overhead in threatening murmurs. About eleven at night the heavy rain drops began to descend—they increased to astonishing violence and about 12 the storm was at its heigth.

The heavy tent cloths flapped about like thread under the violent power of the wind,—the water ran down from the hills in streams passing through the blankets—robes—baggage etc which

[9] After his second expedition, Frémont left his animals at Westport Landing, later reporting, "The animals I had left on pasture were in fine condition; hardened by the previous journey and thoroughly rested they were well fitted to endure a campaign." John Charles Frémont, *Memoirs of My Life*, 424.

[10] The quotes indicate the word was unfamiliar. In the manuscript it is difficult to determine whether the first vowel is "a" or "o." The printer usually makes it "caral." Corral, a yard or enclosure, came to mean a circular pen built of wooden rails set on posts. Ramon F. Adams, *Western Words*, 76.

impeeded its progress. The tents afforded no security against the water, though they warded off the descending rain, and the poor voyagers who lay crouched like a flock of partridges beneath them, felt their bedclothes and their apparel become wet & heavy. They however were not to be pitied, when we say that many, unable to find a place within the tents, had been compelled to spread their blankets in the open air and in the empty uncovered waggons. These were of course forced to bear patiently the pitiless pelting of the storm—and to be kept awake by the continual glare of the sheet lightning which lighted up the prairie equal to a noon day sun. Amongst this latter class was the unfortunate François.— he lay crouched in the corner of an uncovered wagon, his gun lay by him and his baggage was strewn around. Another individual there was at the other end of the waggon—but he—fortunate fellow,—slept & snoozed away in the rain, as if on a bed of warm feathers. He no doubt was used to such fare—and had been in a thousand storms like this, for he was a Canadian voyageur.

Some, were kept on foot—and one poor fellow stalking about in the mud and rain, without shoes and asking in a pitiful voice for information concerning the whereabouts of his hat which the wind no doubt had borne away, looked not unlike some unfortunate ghost among the ruins of Babylon or Colma on the hill of Storms.

Thus passed the first night at Boone's Fork.

"It is night, I am alone, forlorn on the hill of Storms. The wind is heard on the mountain. The Torrent pours down the Rock. No hut receives me from the rain; forlorn on the hill of winds!"

The Songs of Selma.

CHAPTER TWO

In which the Reader becomes marvellously edified concerning divers things & classes of persons.

THE morning following the storm last described, the ruddy sun arose bright and warm and seemed willing to repay the half-drowned wretches on Boone's Fork for the inconveniences which they had suffered, by infusing into them the following day, a most cheering and comfortable degree of warmth. The men spread out their blankets and clothing to the sun's rays—wiped the damp and rust from their guns, and long before the sun was preparing to again descend below the west, they evinced by their quick motions that their sprightliness of which the tempest had momentarily deprived them, was returned in full force.—Another shelter was reared—the men to whose numbers there was an increase of some 20 or 30 others by this time—were divided off into messes of 7 & 8, and to these were distributed provisions and the necessary utensils to prepare them for use.—Bread—Crackers—Bacon—sugar & Coffee—together with tin pans—Cups—Coffee Boilers & fry pans.

The consequence of these distributions became soon manifest— The crackers were soon devoured—fires were made—and whilst some sat around and gazed at the preparations around them, There were some cutting and frying meat,—others with their arms in dough and flour up to the elbow, and others again browning and grinding coffee. Truly it was a time of Cooks and Cooking.

Whilst the camp was being increased each day by the arrival of new bands or groups of engagés, the Capt. and his aids were

10

not idle.—Mules and horses were purchased for the use of the company,—Waggons were bought and put into a condition for immediate use,—Tents were being manufactured—The provisions were stowed into sacks to the amount some 60 or 80 weight in order for packing, whilst the animals were quietly herding out on the prairie and feeding on the splendid grass in order to prepare themselves unconsciously for the trip before them.

The loafering portion of the little army, occupied themselves in shooting at a mark. (by the way—they were mostly proficients), hunting rabbits along the little creek. (Boone's Fork)—fishing for cats & sunfish,—and mounting a mule now & then and scampering across the prairie in pursuit of some scapegrace mule or horse.

Before many days had gone by the company were divided into guards for the purpose of drilling them for the journey ahead.

The guard of the last night watch was always that of the following day—and it was their business to drive the animals at day break out of the enclosure or caral into the prairie, and there to watch over them, so that none might wander, untill dusk—when they would again drive them into the caral—and be relieved by the first watch.

Mounting a mule and gallopping over the green slopes was at first great amusement for those green & verdant ones who were yet fresh and innocent,—but after they had passed a whole day, on horseback out on the prairie, in a heavy, seorching rain,—during which it is very necessary that the guard keep awake,—for it is the nature of a band of mules to turn their backs to the storm and travel before it if not prevented, and even then it frequently happens that they will not heed any attempt to obstruct their passage, but will one & all dash forward with curved neck & erect ears,—snorting & kicking, in one immense band & gallop like a tornado over the distant swells, after spending a day interspersed with such scenes, I repeat, the greenhorns soon become heartily disgusted with mule guarding, & mule riding, & if they had not been forced as it were to guard in their turn, I doubt much whether any of them would have felt willing to volunteer his services for such duty, even though the mules take a stampede[1] and travel off a hundred miles.

Some mules there were too, which entertained as great abhorrence for being rode, as the class of which I just spoke, did for riding them, now it was a solemn fact that these same mules did try all kinds of modes & manners wherby to ease themselves of their oppression and their rider at the same time. One would put on a most ferocious air when approached with a bridle and snort most terrifically as if he had never seen a bridle. Another would not submit to be led but must needs turn his head in a contrary direction and make off, frequently with bridle—halter—and greenhorn. Another would swell himself when girt, and afterwards slip from under the saddle, thereby pitching his sage rider head over heels on the grass. Others again would clinch the bridle bit like a vice, between their teeth and then make off, in spite of everything greenhorn could do or say. Some would not go at all.—Others would go too fast, and some would be very quiet and peacable untill mounted & then there would ensue a series of snortes, lunges, whirlings, kickings, & whizzings, which might vie with any of the performances of the classic Bucephalus.[2]

These same mules by the way be tremendous stout in the neck,— a common little Spanish mule can make off with a strong rope tied about his neck & a greenhorn holding on to the end, at the rate of about 8 miles per hour. and I have frequently noticed mules flying across the hills and hollows with 5 & 6 stout greenhorns holding

---

[1] Stampede or Stampado, a Mexican word applied by them to that picturesque yet terrific manoeuvre exhibited by a band of wild horses when terrified by any approaching object. With expanded nostril—erect ear—and flowing mane & tail— head high in the air, the terrified animals start off like the wind & soon disappear over the prairie.—Montaignes' note.

[2] The war horse of Alexander the Great.

on to his Cabresse.[3] The success of mules in these instances was not to [be] wondered at, for there is great slight[4] in keeping their heads toward you—and there is great danger from their heels, which cause wounds equal to strokes from a Bowie knife. There were some mules too which were difficult of approach,—for on whichever side a greenhorn would approach, on that side would he come in contact with the mule's heels instead of his head. There were others again which could not suffer to be tickled in the ribs by spurs and these would likewise try all diabolical and cunning tricks to throw their riders. One instance of this latter kind I well remember & will narrate it even now, as illustrating most forcibly both to us and to the greenhorn in question, the fact that some mules are ticklish.

Sam—Ike[5] and Zeek[6] being guards for the day, mounted a like number of diminutive but stout mules and set forth to guard the herd.

Sam and Ike by chance were mounted on patient and good hearted quadrupeds—but it happened to Zeek's mortification that his mule was almost a little too low and short in the legs. Zeek's legs were remarkably lengthy and hung down below the mule's belly like a brace of tow-lines.

We had been out for some 3 or 4 hours—when, Zeek's mule becoming tired no doubt with the weight he bore, began to move about less brisk than at first. Hereupon Zeek esteeming it his duty to spur up his ambition, quietly drew up one leg & applied his armed heel to the sides of said mule. This was done as quietly as

---

3 Cabresse. A sort of rope, made by Indians from the hide of a buffaloe,—they cut it into long slits or strings and plat them. They are about the thickness of a man's finger and very stout. They are of various lengths, from 10 to 40 feet.—Montaignes' note. ["Cabresse" may be a corruption of *cabestro*, Spanish for "halter," which came to mean a horsehair-rope halter rather than one of leather or rawhide; see Adams, *Western Words*, 49.]

4 "Slight" in its less-common meaning of carelessness.

5 "Ike" possibly is Isaac Cooper, alias Montaignes.

6 "Zeke" in *The Western Journal*, but consistently "Zeek" in the manuscript.

13

could have been done, But before Zeek's leg returned fairly to its stirrup—Zeek himself was cast heels over head like lightning & the mule sped away to join his comrades. This fall not being from any considerable heigth, was however accompanied with some little feelings of surprise in Zeek's mind, and it was some time before he recovered his mind so far as to go & catch his animal again. There existed in Zeek's mind however a sort of doubt as to the cause which occasioned his headlong descent, and he resolved to plant himself with much firmness in the saddle and try the manoeuvre again. Without more ado therefore he grasped the pommel of the saddle with one hand, and applied his heel for the second time to the mule's ribs. This action however was attended with a more rapid effect than the first, and Zeek felt himself going through the air with great violence. His head struck the soil first, and his long body rearing itself erect for a moment, bottom upwards, at last fell to the ground . . . Zeek picked himself up.

However he was well convinced this time that the fault was his—and not unwilling to behold some farther trial, but not at his own expense, he quietly offered the spur to Baptiste[7] who, at this time came to relieve him. "He is rather lazy, Baptiste and you better take this spur." Baptiste took the spur & buckled to his heal. He mounted muly & dug his heels into his side as a preparatory step. This had better not have been done however for Baptiste fared the same as Zeek. his head sunk into the yielding turf. —Baptiste wanted no greater inducements, and he took off the spur.

---

[7] Possibly Baptiste Tesson, who had accompanied Frémont on his second expedition. George Bird Grinnell has this note about him: "In 1844 a Frenchman named Tesson who was employed at [Bent's] Fort shot at the Negro blacksmith, because he had been charivaried the night before [by a party of men including the blacksmith]. He missed the Negro [but] because he was a passionate and dangerous man Captain St. Vrain gave him an outfit and sent him away from the fort." Grinnell, "Bent's Old Fort and Its Builders," *Kansas Historical Society Collections*, Vol. XV (1919–22), 56.

To say all in a few words,—of all devil's tricks and diabolical modes of whirling—wheeling—whizzing—sneezing—snorting—& kicking—these same mules tried the most approved models . . . .

They were mostly old Mexican and Californian animals, who had served in former campaigns—were well acquainted with all the mysteries of pack saddles and packs—and had long before this, no doubt, come to the conclusion that such things were nuisances and ought to be dispensed with. They had numerous scars on their backs & sides and wished not to be scarified more.

There were also many American horses and young untried and intractible mules which it was necessary to break for the saddle previous to starting. There were 2 or 3 Mexican Spaniards in our camp,—filthy beings without doubt, but complete masters of the noble science of horsemanship, and on these devolved the task of mounting such unruly animals as disdained the saddle. Many a fall had the poor greenhorns who attempted to vie with them, and even one of the Mexicanos themselves, poor fellow, experienced a heavy fall from a horse, which kept him from mounting another for several days.

Whilst encamped on this creek of Boone's Fork, which we were during two weeks, there ensued a series of rains and tempests, which from their duration and disagreeableness, we were indeed to consider as inauspicious of the Expedition which was underweigh.

The little creek abovementioned would rise to the depth of 6 or 8 feet in a short time and frequently whilst the animals would be feeding out, some distance from camp, their return would be delayed and almost prevented by the rain swelling the rivulets which intervened between them and the camp. The caral happened to be close to the banks of the creek,—and it was no great matter of surprise therefore that the camp was compelled to turn out one midnight, in order to free the animals from the overflowed caral.

15

Finally after waiting at the inhospitable camping place until all whom he had engaged to accompany him across the mountains had collected, and everything was prepared for a start, Capt Frémont ordered the mules and horses to be lassoed and every man to be apportioned an animal for the saddle and one or more in addition to carry the packs, of which he had care. On the evening of the 22nd June, therefore the animals were driven into a caral prepared for the purpose, at an early hour, and with ropes in their hands, every man took possession of a brace of animals. There was much running and racing, kicking etc, of course, but by this time the men were used to such things, and the mules & horses were, one and all, haltered and led out to the hills and there picketed.

CHAPTER THREE

Wherein the great North—Western—American—mule—and—packsaddle—Exploring—Expedition makes a grander move than was ever made before, and the mules themselves take a notion to make the grandest move of all.—The Effect of which moves is awful, and the like has never been seen before nor will ever be seen again.

MORNING.—mules caught—packs—divers amusing circumstances—viz. kicks and bites,—snorts and tumbles.—Blinding and tying mules in order to pack them.—François's marvellous good luck. viz. in getting the wildest and most ferocious animal of the crowd.—grand display—awful start.—The Caravan En Route.—a horrible ditch full 3

16

inches deep and a foot wide causes a 6 mule team to falter, whereat certain devilish quadrupeds yclept mules become terrified and slide their packs and riders very decently overhead and then slide off themselves.—François mule among the balance performs sundry military evolutions around him, and that too, with such exceeding science and velocity as to free himself of his own pack by reason of centrifugal forces—and free him from François' power,—who, alarmed at such manifest audacity, looses all holds, and descends, saddle and all to the sod.—after which the pack mule makes off over the hill leaving the packs to take care of themselves. Awful hot pursuit.[1]

All things being in readiness for a start, as has been narrated in the last chapter, about 10 o'clock on the 23rd day of June 1845, Captain Frémont issued orders to catch up and saddle. Then ensued a scene which, for its action and novelty exceeded all description. Here & there were loose mules, running like streaks of daylight across the prairie with long ropes trailing on behind them, and at the end an iron picket every now and then striking their heels and spurring them onward,—There also, would be another group of some 4 or 5, pulling a stubborn mule into camp,—whilst far away on the prairie might be discerned some unfortunate wight vainly endeavoring to resist the onward impetus instilled into his belly by his run away mule. Old—experienced hands at the profession had apparently an easy time of it.—They were mostly judges of mules,—i.e. they knew which had been used the most & which therefore were the tamest & would submit the easiest. When, however, they came across a violent mule in their mess, they did nothing more than run a

---

[1] Of this two-paragraph summary of Chapter Three, *The Western Journal* retained only the following: "Wherein the Great northwestern-mule-wagon and pack-saddle Exploring-Expedition makes a grand movement, and its historian, one still more grand, though rather mixed with Geometry." The rest of the chapter shows only casual resemblance to Montaignes' manuscript.

couple of ropes around his legs, and after throwing him to the ground,—would tie a handkerchief around his eyes and secure the saddle & pack to him whilst down.—the tame ones were an easy task and by one o'clock, the whole was ready.

First came the little carriages, with square black roof bearing the Captain's baggage and instruments[2]—drawn by 2 mules— The Captain and Campmaster generally preceded this—whilst next in order came a 4 mule waggon with a red cover.—then came another similar vehicle,—close in the rear of this came Winright's team, likewise drawn by 4 mules—and after this,—bringing up, the extreme rear of the waggon trains was the 6 mule team of Wise & Breckenrige.[3] Now in the rear of this team there came a great crowd of loose horses and mules, kept within certain bounds by several horsemen who skirmished around them,—There followed next a long train of men on horseback,—leading pack-mules—some one—some 2 & some even 3. Some likewise led spare horses.[4]

The day was fine and sunny and the cavalcade as soon as

[2] Says *The Western Journal* version: "a little Yankee waggon (upon springs), for all the world like those we have seen with cargoes of clocks and of tinware, having a square black top with its curtains buttoned down behind and on each side . . . laden to the top with an endless variety of sextants, circles, telescopes, microscopes, thermometers, barometers, chronometers, etc., etc. In a word, all the principal contrivances for making a complete survey of the whole country: one perfectly botanical, geological, astronomical, historical and zoological, including every scientific item from the domestic economy of the prairie dog to an analysis of the Great Salt Lake." This is typical of the expanded verbiage in *The Western Journal* and raises questions about the reliability of the added data. Frémont planned no such "complete survey." He says, in *Memoirs*, 425: "It was getting late in the season. The principal objects of the expedition lay in and beyond the Rocky Mountains, and for these reasons no time could be given to examinations of the prairie region. The line of travel was directed to pass over such country as would afford good camping-grounds; where water and grass, and wood and abundant game would best contribute to maintain the health of the men and the strength of the animals."

[3] *The Western Journal* omits the names of Winright, Wise, and Breckenridge. In Frémont's fourth expedition, a man named Wise discarded his gun and blanket "and a few hundred yards farther fell over into the snow and died." Cardinal Goodwin, *John Charles Frémont*, 166.

[4] At this point, an installment of Chapter Three in the December, 1852, issue of *The Western Journal* ends, to be concluded in the January, 1853, issue.

formed, got under motion; In tolerable order it proceeded over the first hill or butte, & then, there happened the first difficulty which although trivial, nevertheless caused no little discomfiture to certain persons who had the charge of wild mules. The waggon driven by Marion Loise[5] being heavily laden, sank deeper into the soft soil then the rest, and having to cross a little ditch or ravine ploughed by descending rain across the road, the mules faltered, and the wheels imbedded themselves firmly in the mud. The team of course remained in the middle of the road. As the balance of the caravan passed on, it entered the brain of several mules to make the mired waggon a suitable object to become scared at and thus afford a good pretence for a row. Several therefore gave a snort or two and threw their packs—some cast their rider overhead, whilst the mule of François which happened to be a very devil, and had to be knocked down with a stone before he would submit himself to be caught,—became frightened like the rest and commenced a series of evolutions around his master, which would have surprised Euclid himself, if he had not known that the mule could have described circles with a rope as a radius and a greenhorn as a centre, with as much surity as any geometrician with a pair of compasses. The unsophisticated François supposing it to be a mere show or joke on the mule's part, humoured his caprices for some time, and wheeled his own riding mule around for several times; But percieving after some half-a-dozen turns, that the other was but increasing in the violence of his motions and had already freed himself from his loose pack by the extraordinary centrifugal force of his wheeling motion, he wisely loosed the rope from around the pommel of his saddle and suffered the rascal to escape, which he did, snorting like some wild beast at a menagerie and disappearing over the hill with the fleetness of an antelope,—the packsaddle still secured to him. François's own saddle turned at the same moment and he

[5] *The Western Journal* omits the name of Marion Loise.

came to the ground. Such was the youth's first debut on the Stage of Prairie Life.

He however was but one of many such: The whole path from our camp on Boone's Fork to the place where we pitched our second camp, on the Blue itself, was but a long line of scattered waggons & packmules,—mules with packsaddles on their backs and the packs themselves gone—dismounted greenhorns,—and packs lying in the road.

The distance from 1st camp to the 2nd on Blue was but 6 miles, but during the time we were travelling it, an experienced hand could have packed 3 mules and driven them 12.

We took the road called the Santa Fé or Spanish Trace for our guide—and the reader must be informed that we retained it, untill we reached Pawnee Fork some 300 miles distant.[6]

At this 2nd camp—on Blue as I have said—we remained the balance of that day—the whole of the 2 next, and half of the next. So that it was about 12 o'clock on the 26th, before we got fairly started on our journey across the plains.

During our sojourn here, however, there happened several circumstances, the particulars of which I must fain narrate to the reader.

We picketed our mules and horses out in the grass for the night—and pitched our tents; for the aspect of the heavens forboded rain. The[y] spoke well it seemed for it commenced drizzling in the night and did not cease the next day except for small intervals. Wood and water had to be transported from a distance, but we managed well enough to afford generally a good fire and

[6] Josiah Gregg, *Commerce of the Prairies* (ed. by Max L. Moorhead), 217, lists Pawnee Fork as 298 miles from Independence. The Pawnee River flows into the Arkansas near the present Larned, Kansas. The camp on the Blue is more puzzling, since the Blue or Big Blue River flows into the Missouri east of Westport. Upper branches turn westward below present Kansas City, so the expedition may have moved southward to strike the Blue or one of its branches. The Blue is not mentioned in *The Western Journal.*

plenty at meals. By the orders of the Captain several beeves were driven along with us, and today one of them was slaughtered, the meat being distributed in equal shares to the different messes. Several additional hands arrived at this camp and amongst the rest came 2 waggons, drawn by oxen, in which a large part of our plunder & provisions were to be transported over the yielding loam untill we should reach such soil as to allow the narrow wheeled waggons belonging to the company to receive their proper loading.

The day following our arrival at this camping-place François and others took a hunt along the woods which border the stream called Blue, and as this was swollen to some depth by the rains,— it became necessary for François to wade it several times. This was no inconvenience to him however, for he was well aware he would have to ford worse crossing streams than the Blue, although then he knew not how often he would have to wade the Arkansas.[7] There was nothing to kill, however, in this country, for the Shawnees run every deer out of it and shoot every rabbit or squirrel they see.

There were several fields enclosed with rail fences in the bottoms, and 2 or 3 Indian houses—but no Indians. Several Shawnees appeared at camp today (24th) but they came only to sell some vegetables. The men employed themselves in hunting, fishing etc—although they shot nothing & caught little yet they were still buoyant & sanguine & prepared to pack up and start at a moment's notice.

During the night of the 24th, an individual who was nominally the guard at the time, was found asleep in a tent and was conse-

---

[7] The reference to future crossings of the Arkansas indicates that the manuscript is not a daily journal kept during the expedition. *The Western Journal* interpolates a story that François, terming himself "our modern Mike Fink," waded the Blue while stalking what he supposed to be a bear. His shot put a hole through the blackened stump of a tree.

quently reported the following day to the Commander in Chief. Nothing was said at the moment, but during the course of the day, a proclamation was made through camp for the

"Long hair'd Greeks to Come to Council."[8]

The men assembled one and all at the Captain's tent, not knowing what was going to be done, when he abruptly opened the subject by informing us that a man on guard had fallen asleep, and that he was to quit his service immediately etc. he did not wish to have sleepy guards in his camp, etc.

He then turned the subject to the keeping of journals and declared his intention to have no journals kept in his camp "For["] said he, ["]I'll do my own writing." He then wound up by telling us one and all to keep our mouths shut about our route, our designs etc, for no one but himself, should know. He then declared Martial Law to be the Law of His Camp.[9]

At this point of his debate, there was a manifest shaking of heads and some ten or eleven individuals displeased at his tone towards the men in general, immediately marched up to his tent, returned their arms & received their discharges. A waggon was then in camp, ready to return to Westport, and the services of this, they immediately chartered. Throwing their possible sacks into it, they seated themselves into it & with a huzzah they left Frémont. Many wished afterwards they had gone too! The Captain gazed after them untill they disappeared and then turning to his black servant who acted in the capacity of Valet-de-Chambre, "Those men will be laughed at, when they reach Saint Louis."[10] Mesty-Woolah grinned entirely round his head. To add to the

8 The quotation is from Homer's *Iliad*.

9 In *The Western Journal*, Frémont's speech is expanded with quite apparent intent to put it in an unfavorable light.

10 The departure of "some ten or a dozen" men appears in Chapter IV in *The Western Journal*. The sleeping sentinel, previously called Dogberry (the constable in *Much Ado about Nothing*), now appears as "the unfortunate Dogberry or Verges, whatever his name was."

formidable appearance of his company—Captain Frémont distributed out to them 50 pair of tremendous horsepistols with shining barrels and rusty holsters. There consequently ensued great contests, as to who could hit the side of a board, with one of these formidable firearms, at 5 steps distant. The company fired some 2 or 3 hundred shots at a large box-cover 5 steps distant but to their great surprise they could not only not make any hole in it, but couldn't even form an idea as to the probable direction which the ball may have taken at its discharge from the barrel. The magnanimous and justly celebrated Commander in Chief however, though not larger than one of these same horsepistols[11] must needs despatch Mesty-Woolah for his pistols in order to show to the admiring eyes of his men, the extraordinary precision with which he could hit a board at 5 steps distance. As Bad Luck would have it however, just as the renowned Captain pulled the trigger and shut his eyes—an enormous dab of mud ploughed up by the ball in its downward coarse struck the centre of the board and proclaimed him victor. Here Mesty-Woolah grinned so, as to make François think his head was about to drop off.

About 12 o'clock on the 26th June we again struck our tents—packed our mules and turned Westward. It rained, but that was a thing we all were by this time pretty well used to. The loose mules attempted to make a row & have a stampede but that would not take, for by this time, we were used to that too. So all things went by smoothly enough. The waggons were all light and the rivulets were not hard to cross. We journied this day but 10 miles & encamped for the 3rd time on the Blue.[12] It is well to notice here

11 Frémont was approximately five feet, two inches tall. There is no mention of the horse-pistol contest—nor of Mesty-Woolah—in *The Western Journal*. Frémont, *Memoirs*, 424, mentions having a dozen rifles in his baggage to be given as prizes to the best marksmen in contests along the way.

12 Again the Blue is not mentioned in *The Western Journal*. This paragraph begins the fourth chapter, which is mainly an expansion of the remainder of the third chapter of the manuscript. A bit about the pickets seems to be the only material addition: "The pickets used by us were principally iron pointed, and round, about

that the waggons were always driven in the form of a circle and our tents placed in such a manner as to add to the circle. In the area enclosed we drove our pickets & secured our mules at dusk and at daylight we turned them loose to graze at pleasure on the outside. At this camp there joined us several more hands—Canadians came to fill the places left vacant by the departure of yesterday. We were yet in the Shawnee country and several individuals of this nation came into our camp with vegetables & butter. Another beef was killed at this place and whatever meat was not devoured soon was prepared for future use by jerking it. i.e. cutting it into thin slices and placing it on a scaffold so as to be smoked by the fire.

The surrounding country presented the appearance of a rolling sea—interspersed with long & endless strips of timber in the valleys, not unlike some Hydra of the Ocean.

Throwing the Lasso.

---

eighteen inches in length, and having a revolving ring attached, about four inches below the head, to receive the rope or halter. A square picket of hard wood is preferable to one of this description, being much more difficult to extract in loose soil, whilst the round one works itself out with every movement of the lariette." For the rest, François expends several paragraphs telling why he has named the previous camp Ursa, or Camp Bear, in honor of his adventure. There is "a word or two" exceeding two hundred about the Canadian engagé, or hired hand.

[Between Chapters Three and Four of the manuscript, the version printed in *The Western Journal and Civilian* interpolates more than three chapters of added material, constituting Chapters V, VI, and VII, appearing in the issues of March, April, and May, 1853 (Volume IX, No. 6, and Volume X, Nos. 1 and 2).

Chapter V is headed "An episode, in which François puzzles himself, as well as the reader, in useless conjectures respecting the object of the Expedition as well as the probable cost thereof." François seeks the why and wherefore of "so large a body of armed men, sufficient to form a small army . . . wagons laden with munitions, ammunition, provisions and equipment of every variety from one of Franenhofer's best refractors to Thomas Gray's patent iron pickets . . . kegs of brandy, pounds of vermilion, and boxes of vermicelli and macaroni . . . 80 men or more, some 200 head of horses and mules." He admits that the enterprise was "gotten up on the most economical scale, some of the men getting *only* $15 and others *only* $75 per month, and the bacon and sugar lasting *only* as far as Pawnee Fork." The italics suggest sarcasm. He estimates the cost at between $40,000 and $60,000, "an inconsiderable sum, to be sure, for a great and wealthy people," but echoes a common criticism of the Pathfinder. The "object cannot be discovery for the simple reason that there is nothing but what *has been discovered*, long ago," he writes, mentioning Lewis and Clark, Pike, Gregg, and the trappers who discovered South Pass. A footnote "for the guidance of the future historian" points out that Major Fitzpatrick led the first band through South Pass in 1824. He also names the Sublettes, Campbell, Vásquez, Ashley, Smith, Bridger, and Walker, names that were rediscovered some years later.

Montaignes concludes that conquest is out of the question because "filibustering is a practice discountenenced and unassisted by our law-abiding government," and, reverting to the pretense of a contemporary journal, declines to resolve the mystery.

25

Next follows Chapter VI, "Wherein François discourseth learnedly concerning the Sahara desert and its Bedouins." He discusses "the barren Llanos or plains of the Great West" and advances a theory about Indians, suggesting that "as the ground gradually increases in elevation, the strange people, who roam over its surface, seem to degenerate accordingly. . . . Whether or not atmospheric pressure has a tendency to encourage the evil propensities of man's nature, is a question too profound for us to touch upon."

The chapter contains some travel notes on the "Santa Fé Road or Trail (as it is called by the traders)," that may be summarized. "Our camp at this spot" presumably was near the Shawnee Missions since he says it was visited by Shawnee hucksters with vegetables and butter, "and as this latter commodity was rather scarce among the democracy, the trade in these luxuries became a monopoly." He designates the site three pages later as Camp Monopoly. Having complained of Frémont's secrecy about the route, François admits that it did not deter him "from dotting down a sufficiency of hieroglyphics of various outlandish forms, to enable him afterwards to locate every spot on the road, by the marvellous association of dot and incident."

The starting point, not only for Santa Fe but also for Oregon or California, was Elm Grove—variously called Round Grove and Lone Elm—at Horse-Shoe Bend. About twelve miles from Lone Elm, the trail crosses Bull Creek, "deriving its name doubtlessly from a great [buffalo] battle" but sometimes confused with Pool Creek farther west. Black Jack Grove, on Black Jack Creek is named for the tree. Willow Spring and Rock Creek are two small tributaries of the Kansas, and One Hundred and Ten is "the first water of the Osage, or as laid down by some, *The Marais des Cygnes*." This is approximately 110 miles from "old Fort Osage,—at present Sibley,—on the Missouri River," and Montaignes notes several times that it is the range of the Kaw or Kansas Indians, "a good-for-nothing and thievish race."

Next crossed are Bridge Creek, Switzer's Creek, and Fish Creek —eighty-eight miles by the viameter from Cantonment Leavenworth. Then comes Pleasant Valley Creek and a camp at Big John Spring on a creek of the same name running into the Neosho or Council Grove Creek, sometimes called Grand River. He mentions Little John, sometimes called Bluff Creek, to the right of the road before Big John is reached. Six miles farther is Council Grove, the last stand of heavy timber before reaching the mountains. Long grass ends there, except in creek bottoms, "whilst the short, crispy buffalo grass, or *Sisleria dactyloides* . . . becomes the sole tenant of the soil." François spends the rest of this installment speculating on how an animal as gigantic as the buffalo can be nourished by such scanty grass.

Chapter VII, entitled "Wherein François taketh a roundabout way to prove axioms; viz: that Indians will steal, and that travellers and explorers will not be believed," continues his speculation on increased elevation advancing degeneracy. A footnote to Chapter VI (pp. 70–71) might be pertinent: "The train of James White, of Independence, Mo., was attacked at the Point of Rocks by a party of Apache Indians, and the entire company barbarously murdered and scalped, excepting Mrs. White and her infant daughter. This unfortunate lady was reserved by the savages for a far more horrible fate, and could her sufferings be realized by the white man who reads the mere detail, his hair would stand on end, and the red man's cause be forever lost in the feeling of revenge. I was well acquainted with Mrs. White and saw her in our city just previous to her departure. . . . the troops . . . found but an amaciated, shattered wreck of what once has been a delicate and refined American female: barbarously mangled and murdered, the blood still oozing from the wounded heart." The note is signed "F. Des M."

In this chapter, however, he mentions only meeting on Cow Creek "several Kickapoos with a drove of good looking horses, obtained at some place they could not recollect where," and he concludes that "Indians WILL steal."

The other promised subject matter is disappointing. The tall tales of a Canadian voyageur are only briefly recounted. He had trapped beaver and been chased by Blackfeet on every stream "flowing into the Columbia, Colorado, Missouri, or Mississippi," including the Texas Cross Timbers by way of the Canadian River, which is a long chase by Blackfeet.

Chapter VIII begins with two pages on the "musquitoes and gallinippers" of Cow Creek and the Big Bend of the Arkansas, but returns to the manuscript narrative with events of July 3 and 4.]

CHAPTER FOUR

Herein are recorded the principal Events which took place from the time we left the Blue, till we crossed Pawnee Fork of Caw or Kanzas River.

OUR usual hour for starting and our usual day's travel, nooning or resting at noon.—the appearance of the travellers over this region. Santa Fé waggons.—men from the mountains.—tales concerning the dangerous proximity of Camanches and Pawnees.—2 Delaware youths.—Council Grove—Cottonwood Creek.—Cow Creek—Kickapoo Indians with horses—Neosho or grand River.—Owl Creek. Meet 14 waggons from Bent's fort on the head waters of the Arkansas—the

drivers—we cross a creek and Camp.— 4th July.—the arrival
of the Santa Fé waggons.—Shooting match for clothing. Brandy
distributed—and arms discharged.—appearance of Buffaloe
Bones,—mosquitoes.—a grave on the plains.—antelope,—the
mode of killing them.—wolves—Badgers—Skunk, or polecat—
prairie dogs—their towns—Burrowing owls—Pawnee Rock—
Bad water,—heavy storm,—tents blow over etc.—5 of us walk the
next day: Pawnee Rock—Jeffer's mishap.—great Spring called
Big John.—Harden kills an antelope—swans or pelicans in the
distance—the Crossing of Pawnee Fork—the waggons return
home the 4th of July.—A mosquito bar shot for on the Arkansas.
—François lies awake 2 nights—bathing in the Arkansas.—the
Caws.—Their rascality—Their greeting of Henry Henry.

Our mules were usually saddled & packed by sunrise and frequently before the bright planet would have his face totally above
the Eastern horizon, our tents would be struck & our caravan
in motion.

Twas our general custom whilst Capt Frémont had the command, to stop about 12 o'clock at some hole or other where there
was water, and remain for an hour and a half—in order to rest
the mules. But in my opinion and in that of those who are well
experienced in such things this was an injurious proceeding. T'is
far better to start early and continue moving, untill your day's
travel is accomplished than to stop half-way—unpack your animal and remain dozing for an hour or so. You deprive your mule
of more than one and a half hour's feeding & rest, and you your-
self, (I'll vouch for the truth of this) feel anything but contented.
We had a fine proof of this on our return under Mr. Fitzpatrick.[1]
We passed through a more arid & barren country than that which
we travelled on our route out, and by following the plan which I

[1] Thomas Fitzpatrick, who guided the Abert expedition from Bent's Fort to St.
Louis. See Chapter Seven.

have noticed, of making but one job out of a day's journey, we usually performed the same distance per diem (about 22 miles on an average) in less time and with less injury and exhaustion to our mules.—The system of nooning also, so much followed by Capt Frémont, is any thing but comfortable or advantageous to the men:—and it is by no means pleasant to be commanded to halt and unsaddle in the middle of an arid prairie, scorched by the hot sun, and there remain during an hour or more, only to be again ordered to pack up and mount.[2]

Before arriving at Pawnee Fork we met several travellers in couples, and sometimes single coming from the mountains,—also an Indian and his squaw.—likewise passing some 8 or ten heavy laden Santa Fé waggons.—Every wayfarer we met was eagerly questioned by us as to his wherefrom & his whitherto! The accounts of these travellers were for the most part, interspersed with awful tales and yarns about Camanches and Pawnees awaiting our arrival at Pawnee Fork.

These accounts were of course, cause of much anxiety to many of us, being so very green as we were, and we expected nothing less on our arrival at the Crossings of Pawnee Fork, than to behold the opposite bank crowded with Indians . . . .[3] After several days of our march, the 3rd of July, 2 Delaware youths[4] joined our Caravan, and were employed to accompany us to Bent's Fort.

[2] "Nooning" was a common practice. Stanley Vestal says, "A caravan usually rested in the heat of the day and travelled only for a few hours . . . early each morning and late in the afternoon." *Wagons Southwest*, 12. Abert and Fitzpatrick eliminated "nooning" on the route back. Instead the caravan remained in camp an hour or two after breakfast, letting the animals graze. Once on the trail, stops were made only in case of accident or upon finding water. Making camp early in the afternoon, they could rest and relax in preparation for the next day's travel. Abert says, "It was afterwards acknowledged that this method of travelling enabled us to accomplish the same distance with much less fatigue to man and beast." *Guádal P'a* (ed. by H. Bailey Carroll), 28.

[3] Four words crossed out and unreadable. They might be "to refuse our passage."

[4] There were, in all, twelve Delaware Indians accompanying the expedition to Bent's Fort. Frémont, *Memoirs*, 424.

We passed Council Grove,[5] which is on the Neosho or Grand River—the stream upon which stands Fort Gibson,[6] saw & drank out of the tremendous spring which goes by the name of Big John[7]—and crossed the Cottonwood Creek[8]—the Cow[9] and Owl Creeks and on the 3rd of July met 14 waggons drawn by oxen and laden with robes from Bent's Fort on the head-waters of the Arkansas.—The drivers of these were a wild looking set.— Creoles—Mexicans & Negroes. They were almost naked and were tanned like Indians. We crossed a small creek and camped.

The following morning was the 4th of July, the anniversary of our Independence. To celebrate it with corresponding gusto the most enthusiastic of the green ones, welcomed daybreak by a volley of fire arms at the Captain's tent. Brandy was served around to them in return and the Captain expressed his intention of remaining at this place the remainder of the day.[10]

The 4th was therefore spent in rest, at least as far as the animals were concerned. The men themselves occupied themselves in various ways—and whilst some bathed, and changed their apparel— others sewed old clothes and towards evening the whole company resolved itself into a shooting match for new ones given as a prize to the nearest shot by the Captain himself. Towards evening the Santa Fé waggons under the conduct of Doan came up.[11]

[5] Trails from various jumping-off places met at Council Grove. Here organization of caravans was completed, and from this point strict discipline was enforced. Stanley Vestal, *The Old Santa Fe Trail*, 31, 32.

[6] Fort Gibson is described in Chapter Eighteen.

[7] Big John Spring, 138 miles from Westport, was a "clear, cool, gushing fountain flowing from the hillside." Vestal, *The Old Santa Fe Trail*, 51.

[8] Cottonwood Creek is a branch of the Neosho River.

[9] Cow Creek flows into the Arkansas.

[10] July 4 celebrations are noted in most trail diaries. Says Josiah Gregg, "This anniversary is always hailed with heart-felt joy by the wayfarer in the remote desert." *Commerce of the Prairies*, 62–63. Stanley Vestal notes that all wagon trains halted wherever they were to celebrate the day. *Wagons Southwest*, 31.

[11] George P. Doan, a Santa Fe trader in partnership with James J. Webb. Louise Barry, "Kansas Before 1854: A Revised Annals," Parts Fourteen and Fifteen, *Kansas Historical Quarterly*, Vol. XXX, Nos. 2–3 (Summer and Autumn, 1964), 231–32, 241, 349, 368.

Our young officers vied with each other after dark, as to who should become the tallest & there ensued some high drinking. —Finding there was not sufficient liquor—an attendant was despatched for more, and it will surprise the Reader when I say that he succeeded in borrowing some.[12]

From this place the 2 ox teams which had accompanied us thus far,—for the purpose of resting our draught mules at least some portion of their route, now turned back towards the States.

The principal thing for which the creeks in this region are famous, is the enormous & irresistible quantum of mosquitoes which infest the tangled bottoms along their banks.

Nothing can resist their fury, & when the indolent cook of the mess proceds after night fall through their region on his way for water, they will attack him in such number & with so much fury & clangour that Cook will be a bold man indeed, if he do not flee.

On Cow Creek for example, we had great difficulty in watering our animals even during day-time, by reason of these same insects. Large flies resembling horse flies likewise abounded. Mosquitoe bars, therefore were in much demand, and it [was] with extraordinary gladness that we heard our Captain give orders to have a regular shooting match for one of these luxuries. Every man hoped that he might win, and as might be expected but one single individual bore away the trophy. 4 more were afterwards shot for on the Arkansas, on the edges of which River, the mosquitoes were as blood thirsty if not more so than any of the small creeks, before mentioned, than the Owl,—Cow—Cottonwood or Neosho—But as in this case like the other only 4 bore away the bars,—this was of no great utility to the company at large. Before reaching the Pawnee Fork,—we passed great quantities of buffaloe skelatons and dead buffaloe lying on the plains and kept looking ahead in expectation of beholding the cheering spectacle of living herds. Although we had as yet seen no buffaloe,

---

[12] which, of course, was never repaid.—Montaignes' note.

we did not suffer for meat, for as I have said, there had been several beeves driven along with us, and we had some amount of bacon.—But the small quantity of flour doled out to us at the first camp, was by this time nearly exhausted, and we expected, if we met no buffaloe soon, to have a lean time of it, with salt meat and coffee.

It is true that we had hunters along with us. i.e men employed for that purpose alone, but the country we were travelling through was but scantily occupied by animals whose meat was fit for use, when there were no buffaloe. The hunters now & then brought in an antelope,—but the meat of this animal is very poor, and it would have required several antelope at a meal to have the rounds of our Camp of 80 men.

There were plenty of wolves—badgers—& prairie* dogs or marmots on these plains & some few skunks or bêtes-puants.—as also many villages of burrowing owls.

---

*The prairie dog or marmot. Charles Lucien Bonaparte, in his Continuation of Wilson's "American Birds" gives the following interesting account of the Burrowing Owl and Prairie Dog.

"venerable ruins crumbling under the influence of time & the vicissitudes of season, are habitually associated with our recollections of the owl; he is considered as the tenant of sombre forests, whose nocturnal gloom is rendered deeper and more awful by the harsh dissonance of his voice. In poetry he has long been regarded as the appropriate concomitant of darkness and horror. But we are now to make the reader acquainted with an owl to which none of these associations can belong; a bird that, so far from seeking refuge in the ruined habitations of man, fixes its residence within the Earth; and instead of concealing itself in solitary recesses of the forest, delights to dwell on open plains, in company with animals remarkable for their social disposition, neatness and order. Instead of sailing forth in obscurity of the morning or

evening twilight, and then retreating to mope away the intervening hours, our owl enjoys the broadest glare of the noon-tide sun,
and flying rapidly along, searches for food or pleasure, during
the cheerful light of day.

In the Trans-Mississippian territories of the United States the
burrowing owl resides exclusively in the villages of the marmot
or prairie dog, whose excavations are so commodious as to render
it unnecessary that our bird should dig for himself, as he is said
to do in other parts of the world where no burrowing animals
exist. These villages are very numerous, and variable in their
extent, sometimes covering only a few acres, and at others spreading over a surface of the country for miles together. They are
composed of slightly elevated mounds, having the form of a
truncated cone, about 2 feet in width at the base, and seldom rising
as high as eighteen inches above the surface of the soil. The
Entrance is placed either at the top or on the side, and the whole
mound is beaten down externally, especially at the summit, resembling a much used foot-path. From the Entrance, the passage
into the mound descends vertically for one or two feet, and is
thence continued obliquely downwards, untill it terminates in
an apartment, within which the industrious marmot constructs,
on the approach of the cold season, the comfortable cell for his
winter's sleep. This cell which is composed [of] fine dry grass,
is globular in form, with an opening at top capable of admitting
the finger; and the whole is so firmly compacted, that it might,
without injury be rolled over the floor.

It is delightful, during fine weather, to see these lively little
creatures sporting about the entrance of their burrows, which are
always kept in the neatest repair, and are often inhabited by
several individuals. When alarmed, they immediately take refuge
in their subterranean chambers; or if the dreaded danger be not
immediately impending, they stand near the brink of the entrance,

bravely barking and flourishing their tails, or else sit erect to reconnoitre the movements of the Enemy.

In all the prairie dog villages the burrowing owl is seen moving briskly about, or else in small flocks scattered among the mounds, and at a distance it may be mistaken for the marmot itself when sitting erect. They manifest but little timidity and allow themselves to be approached sufficiently close for shooting; but if alarmed, some or all of them soar away and settle down again at a short distance; if further disturbed their flight is continued untill they are no longer in view, or they descend into their dwellings, whence they are difficult to dislodge.

The Burrows in which these owls have been seen to descend, on the plains of the Platte (river) where they are most numerous, were evidently excavated by the marmot, whence it has been inferred by many that they were either common, though unfriendly residents of the same habitation, or that our owl was the sole occupant of a burrow, acquired by the right of conquest. The evidence of this was clearly presented by the ruinous condition of the burrows tenanted by the owl, which were frequently caved in, and their sides channelled by the ruins, whilst the neat and well preserved mansion of the marmot showed the active care of a skilful and industrious owner. We have no evidence that the owl and marmot habitually resort to one burrow; yet we are well assured by Pike, and others, that a common danger often drives them into the same excavation where lizards and rattlesnakes also enter for concealment and safety. The owl observed by Villot, in Saint Domingo, digs itself a burrow 2 feet in depth, at the bottom of which its eggs are deposited on a bed of moss—herb stalks and dried roots.

The note of our bird is strikingly similar to the cry of the marmot, which sounds like Cheh, Cheh, pronounced several times in rapid succession; and were it not that the burrowing owls of the West Indies, where no marmots exist, utter the same sound, it might be inferred that the marmot was the unintentional tutor to the young owl; this cry is only uttered as the bird begins its flight. The food of the bird we are describing appears to consist entirely of insects, as on examination of its stomach, nothing but parts of their hardning cases were to be found.["]

The above is very true regarding both the owl and the marmot, but as to remark concerning the owl inhabiting the same burrow with the other, I think that they never do inhabit the same. I have repeatedly noticed that, although we frequently passed villages in which the inhabitants were composed of prairie dogs and owls, yet it was most frequently the case that when we saw a village of burrowing owls—there were none of the former.

The burrows or holes which these same marmots dig often go to decay, when the occupant is killed or forced by enemies to seek another habitation, & in this case the dwelling is immediately taken poss[ess]ion by lizards and rattlesnakes of which there are great numbers; frequently 3 or more in one hole.

The horned frog (crapeau à corne) is also an inhabitant of these plains and many were picked up by the curious and enquiring of our party. Their skin or hide is covered with many sharp pointed horns or thorns, and resembles armour: but these little animals are perfectly harmless.

The Prairie dogs were the cause of some inconvenience to several of the greenhorns, and on the day we passed Pawnee Rock,[13] a famous spot on the Santa Fé Trace, 5 greenhorns were compelled to do penance for killing some of the inhabitants of a marmot village near by, by being made to walk the day following.

There are likewise some skunks or bêtes puants along the hills and many badgers.

We overtook several other Santa Fé waggons before we arrived

---

[13] "Pawnee Rock, sometimes called Painted Rock, or Rock Point, was the most famous landmark of the Santa Fe Trail." This 40-foot high promontary also "served as register of the names of those who passed by." Vestal, *The Old Santa Fe Trail*, 114.

at Pawnee Fork and amongst others were those belonging to Mr. Magoffin.[14] We passed them at Pawnee Rock and had overtaken them at a point where the Arkansas approaches within a mile of the road.

In this company, I saw a young friend, Henry Henry, who was going out to take a peep at Mexico—and see what was going on there.

At our nooning place, several Caw or Kanza Indians came into our camp—sneaking looking vilians.—They are a mean race without doubt—and Henry Henry strengthened me in the opinion I formed of them at first sight, by telling me that whilst riding some 2 or 3 miles ahead of the waggons—these same rascally looking Caws rode swiftly up to him, & would doubtlessly have dismounted & robbed him, if the waggons had not soon come in sight.

The night previous to our arrival at the Fork, was the crisis of a tremendous storm of wind & rain, accompanied by thunder & lightning. From the great level of the prairie the wind had great sweep and soon overturned our tents. Most of us were therefore compelled to hold fast to the ropes to keep it over us & from blowing away. The following day however came out bright & warm and as usual we forgot what took place the last night. The 5 who were ordered to walk, shouldered their rifles & trudged by short cuts across the prairie, taking care to have splendid revenge on every prairie dog that barked at them on their way. Towards one o'clock the foremost reached the eminence from which Pawnee Fork[15] can be seen meandering through the flat plain, and

[14] James Wiley Magoffin and his brother Samuel had been partners in the Santa Fe trade since 1828. In 1846 while Samuel was traveling west with his bride, Susan Shelby, James went alone to Santa Fe on a secret mission. Susan Shelby Magoffin, *Down the Sante Fe Trail and into Mexico*, (ed. by Stella M. Drumm).

[15] Pawnee Fork was a branch of the Arkansas River. "If in flood, it was a difficult stream to cross. . . . when not in flood, was a bold limpid stream that promised a cool drink to the thirsty horseman. . . . known to the Kiowas in early days as Dark Timber River." Vestal, *The Old Santa Fe Trail*, 120–21.

after taking in the carcase of a slaughtered antelope the foremost waggon descended toward the crossings. The banks of this stream were very abrupt and owing to the rain of last night very slippery and bad for the waggons to descend & ascend. However, by the assistance of the men, who dismounted, and pushed the waggons at stern & wheel, the mules drew them safely to the opposite bank —The water at this place was about 2 feet in depth but very swift.

The infantry, at this place, concluding from their own limbs being weary, that it was about time to camp,—made a sort of halt at this crossing, and one cast away his slippers in which he had walked thus far.—But to our surprise and to his consternation the caravan continued in motion untill the last horseman disappeared beneath the horizon. We trudged on manfully however and about 3 o'clock reached the camp about 7 miles from the Fork, extremely exhausted in body and poor Jeffer's feet completely blistered.[16]

A word here respecting the water of this region. In the several small creeks which we crossed—as for example in the Neosho— in the Cow Creek & in the Cottonwood, we found pretty good water—there exist some fine springs along these streams and the finest water I ever drank was out of the spring called Big John. For the most part however, travellers through this country have to drink the rain water which collects in holes and buffaloe wallows and is generally very acid. The water of Pawnee Fork excelled that of any of the other streams which we had crossed. The Arkansas could not compare with it; for though this latter stream

[16] In *The Western Journal* the man who threw away his pumps (slippers in the manuscript) is named Jeams. While the handwriting is not always clear, there seems little doubt that Jeffers is correct. There is also much more detail on the occasion for this punishment—"a furious cannonade" of the prairie dog village that caused Frémont to ride back in expectation of an Indian attack. Basil Lajeunesse, "a favorite companion in former trips, had been included in the proscription." The remainder of this chapter does not appear in the printed version. As another indication that *The Western Journal* printed a revised and edited version, the long quotation from Charles Lucien Bonaparte concerning the prairie dog is replaced by a footnote.

be a mountain torrent and flows from snow covered peaks, yet owing to its wide channel at this place and loose, sandy bed, there was barely sufficient water in it to flow. The sun's rays had full control over it and it was warmer than fresh milk during the day. As to the Indians of this portion of the country there is very little to be said by one at this place. For excepting the 8 or ten Caws or Kanzas of whom I have spoken we saw not another Indian east of Pawnee Fork, excepting 3 or 4 individuals of that roving nation the Kickapoos, whom we met on Cow Creek with a drove of horses.

The grass at this season of the year was splendid in this country and our animals fared well as long as it lasted. T'was a long coarse grass and in many places grew very large & rank. We had not as yet reached the plains where buffaloe grass alone predominates and draws a scanty sustenance from the parched and gravelly soil. There is a species of esculant root grass on the swells of this prairie, the taste of which is very agreeable, It is called by the Canadians—Pommes de Terre.—Ground apple.— It resembles in shape a small turnip.

CHAPTER FIVE

Which transports the Author and Reader by Short but not Easy Stages from Pawnee Fork to Smoky hill Fork.

THERE being no signs of buffaloe, we leave the Spanish Trail & strike off towards the right.— A buffaloe bull seen in the distance about 12 o'clock.—Archambeaux and Frémont make an onslaught upon him with pistols.— Bull shows very good fight—Victory of the whites at the end.—

39

during the combat Frémont loses an elegant pistol.—We continue up Pawnee Fork.—Plenty of good water in its channel and many little ponds on the plains caused by the Late Rains.—numerous villages of prairie dogs or marmots—a herd of buffaloe sunning afar off—Our hunters among them.—Meat brought into Camp—We pitch our Camp near an old Indian Encampment.—Officers and hunters go out on a buffaloe chase.—Many buffaloe around camp.—Enormous gluttonizing on buffaloe meat.—What are called choice pieces—jerking it—Appearance of the surrounding country the day following our departure from the Spanish Trail.—Chasing them on horseback.—frequent falls of greenhorns—danger from wounded buffaloe.—Archambeaux and Lajeunesse lose a fine horse and mule, with saddles,—holsters,—bridles & equipments by leaving them standing on the prairie while they went to attack a distant band of buffaloe.—The buffaloe in their flight pass near the 2 aforesaid animals—and the latter take the Stampede along with them.—The forlorn appearance of the 2 unhorsed hunters in the Camp.—The Captain of one of the guards found asleep during his guard, and his sentence for this misdemeanor.—Rouchou and Lajeunesse are sent out to ascertain if possible the whereabouts of the runaway horse & mule.—Their failure,—Their exceeding panic and conduct, when they saw Capt Frémont & several of his men,—riding furiously over the hills towards them, disguised and yelling like wild Indians.—The panic in Camp at their return.—mules driven and men under arms.—Bad water.—A bridge across the fork,—Bois de Vache or buffaloe dung.—Our Camp is fired upon during night by a party of Indians.—they are supposed to be Pawnees. —Smokey hill Fork.

Our provisions, i.e our sugar & coffee, for we had nothing else, beginning to taper into rather small proportions—and there not being much prospect of arriving at Buffaloe along the travelled route, we therefore on the 16th or 17th,[1] left the Spanish Trail and struck off in a direction west, keeping up the stream called Pawnee Fork, along whose banks, we hoped to behold plenteous herdes of bison before many hours. We had not travelled far before our hopes were realized, we were not as yet out of sight of the territory we had pitched our last camp at, when a small black speck was seen about 4 miles distant on the level and flowing plain.

"A Buffaloe Bull! A Buffaloe Bull" was shouted from every one's lungs, and the dark speck or buffaloe was plainly noticed to be in motion. Soon another dot or speck was added to the view, and the green-horns rubbed, and strained their eyes to make out more in the distance, like the child counting stars. For every one that was counted, 3 more appeared close by which were at first undiscernable.

Archambeaux[2] the main hunter was now called to the front,— and a council ensued between him and the leader. The result was soon apparent; for the 2, well equipped with shot-guns & pistols & mounted on active horses—spurred over the plain, to make an attack on the nearest bull. We continued on our march, yet from the evenness of the plain, the contest between the tremendous animal who formed as it were, the advanced guard of those tremendous phalanxes of bisons towards the west, and the 2 individuals who were seeking his death, only for their own gratification, was plainly discernible, and well watched by us.

The lordly animal moved not, nor appeared to notice them till they were nearly upon him, and then, lifting his head for a

---

[1] "On or about the 17th of July" is the phrase in *The Western Journal*, in which Chapters X, XI, and XII parallel Five in the manuscript, interspersing many general observations designed presumably to amuse the reader, although not too successfully. The opening summary of contents is again omitted.

[2] Archambeaux, the Canadian hunter, is described as "a general favorite. . . . tall, fine looking, very cheerful, with all the gaiety of the voyageur." Since he accompanied Frémont to California, he is not mentioned in Abert's report or in the last half of Montaignes' journal. Edwin Legrand Sabin, *Kit Carson Days*, 389.

moment from his feed, he scanned them with an enquiring eye and then wheeled. It requires a swift horse to come along side of a buffaloe, & though they appear bulky and awkward, yet in their stampede over a prairie they are soon hidden by the horizon. The present animal commenced his flight at too late a moment however and before he had taken many steps, the pistols were discharged against him. He would then wheel around towards his enemies, only to receive an additional rake, untill he was wounded in such a manner as to make him frantic.—The present horsemen were poor shots with a pistol it seemed, for they must have fired some 20 odd balls into the beast before he fell. A shout rent the air, as he fell, from our band and in the course of an hour the victors returned to the camp—minus an elegant pistol lost by the Captain during the heat of the conflict.

We proceded up the stream which I have introduced to my readers by the name of Pawnee Fork of Caw or Kansas River, and finding plenty of good water deposited by the clouds in the little flats of the prairie—we stopped to noon at one of these little ponds—and eat our last meat without bread.[3]

As there were numerous droves of buffaloe in sight—the hunters were sent out to kill some for meat, & about one o'clock, we hitched up and proceeded on our way.—Passing through numerous towns of prairie-dogs or marmots, which, seemed from the loud clamours with which the inhabitants greeted our approach, to be well populated we finally pitched our camp on a small creek, (I doubt whether it be the Pawnee Fork or one of its branches), at a place wherat in former times there must have been a great Indian encampment; thousands of tent poles and sticks upon which they dried their meat, lay around in great quantities.[4]

---

[3] In *The Western Journal*, Montaignes calls the meat, "the last fragment of our much injured middling" and aims this sarcastic jibe at Frémont: "Here again we cannot but pause and reflect upon those profound powers of calculation which could have foretold to a day, to a fraction of a day, the complete annihilation of our rations simultaneously with the appearance of the abundance which herded around us."

The hunters had great success, and mules laden with choice pieces of meat were continually coming into the camp. As soon as our tents were stretched the officers who belonged to our troop, in company with the hunters, set out on a grand buffaloe chase and returned not before dark. They likewise succeeded admirably and, untill a late hour that night, the campfires threw their bright gleam far & wide, and the scaffolds built near them presented rich supplies of fat meat jerking for future use.

It is astonishing, what quantities of this meat, men can devour without feeling any inconvenience. They were all pressed, I shall not say severely, by hunger, and having no bread or any thing else to supply its place, but coffee, the men set to, and commenced a furious onslaught upon the buffaloe meat, as if to make up for lost time and days passed with empty craws. Huge roasts, such as would be placed by a Missouri hostess for 4 men's meal were spitted and stuck near the fire; the men sitting by, with a butcher knife, anxiously awaiting the part nearest the blaze to brown, untill the entire piece would be anhilated. This would not be all, 2 or 3 immense ribs by no means spare of meat, would be next compelled to pass muster, until either there was some inimical opposing complaint or the jaws of the masticator began to work with pain. Whereupon if not on guard, the hero or heroes rolled up in their robes and blankets & turned in for a nap. Such was the principal feauture of the scenery by night amongst the buffaloe on Pawnee Fork.

Not knowing how soon we might be out of such paradisical regions,—And perfectly ignorant how many days would bring us into dry & uninhabited lands flowing with nought but air instead of fat-roasts & sweet ribs, we judged it prudent to lay a good supply of the latter into our inner man, previous to leaving such

---

4 *The Western Journal* adds: "These afforded us a magnificent wood yard to draw upon, and within a few minutes after halting, the fires were kindled in every direction."

43

good quarters, as also to prepare by jerking, as much as possible, to serve in pressing occasions which might happen in future.

Our Chief appeared in no ways anxious about this, as his own larder was already & had always been full, & was so well provided for, as to free him from all fear of the times to come, and, t'was therefore no matter for wonder when he ordered to catch up & saddle.[5]

However, our passage through these plains so well stocked with bison, occupied us longer than we imagined to our joy, and for several days, a whole week, the country through which we wended our way, was in every side for leagues around, black with buffaloe,—2. 3– 4– 5– and 600 in a herd, fighting, feeding—running & racing. Many were killed for meat—and many for whatever gratification it might afford the slayers and our route through them might have been known by the frequent carcasses left on the plains. Many a veteran bull fell beneath our rifles and the savage people of these desert and untillable tracts can not be censured for detesting the whitefaces, who pass through the only pastures with which nature has gifted him, & slay his cattle which feed therein & which form his only means of subsistence— which give him his meat,—his ornaments—his armament and his clothing.

When such numbers were slaughtered, it could not be expected that all the meat could be saved, & consequently the hunters were not very particular.—They generally cut out the tongue, took a part of the tallow and cut off the hump or bosse, which is esteemed a luxury among mountaineers, and left the balance to be devoured by the wolves and buzzards of which there are great quantities.

Though chasing them on horseback, be the mode followed by the Indians mostly, if not altogether, and is much in vogue among the many, yet, I have noticed that the plan followed by wise and

[5] In Frémont's defense it might be said that the party was to remain in buffalo country for several days, a fact that he may reasonably be supposed to have known.

good hunters, who approach them unperceived on foot, and shoot them down at leisure, is generally, far the surest and the neatest plan.

For example, in our route up, that is out west, under Frémont, chasing them on horseback with shot gun & pistol, was the only mode followed: The number of buffaloe, consequently, was much less, considering the quantity of men, than those killed during our homeward trip across the American Desert, when we had no suitable horses in our whole Cavajarde. Without considering the waste of ammunition,—the injury done to the horses,—the insurity of aim, and the danger to be apprehended which is the effect of the former system,—I think that the latter is far the more preferable and most successful.[6]

The prairie Indians.—The Tannus—The Pawnees—The Arapahoes—The Chiennes—The Cayquas—The Camanches and the Apaches,—have few or no fire arms equal to the rifle among them, and could not therefore be expected to enjoy the benefit of the mode first mentioned, and it is but natural for them to follow the only plan in their power. viz. of dashing into a herd,—selecting a fat one, and riding by the side of it discharging arrows into its side untill it falls. As to the danger, which I have noticed as to be apprehended, in chasing buffaloe on horseback, there exist several circumstances which, if not taken heed of will be followed by some injury to the horse or the rider.

For instance, a buffaloe horse as he is technically called is trained in such a manner as to evade all attempts of the infuriated

6 Abert also discusses buffalo hunting from a stand: "When a hunter succeeds in approaching a herd undiscovered he can often kill as many as 10 or 15 without 'raising' the band. They pay very little attention to their fallen companions, unless an unsuccessful shot strikes and wounds one that communicates his fright to the rest of the band. The bulls and calves are scarcely ever used. The former are sometimes killed in the spring, but at all other seasons their flesh is said to be rank and unpleasant. In shooting the cow the hunter always selects the fattest in the band . . . . The cow is smaller and her hair more uniform in length, as well as the diameter of the horn, which in the bull varies rapidly. By this the sexes are easily distinguished, even by a glance at the skull, many of which we examined." *Guádal P'a*, 57–59.

buffaloe, to gore him, and will keep out of his reach, yet close enough at the same time to allow his rider to shoot him. Most of the prairie Indians' horses are thus trained. Now an American steed, or one which has never seen buffaloe and consequently has never chased them, will generally dash forward towards them untill he see sufficient of the enemy to frighten him, and then, away he'll go in spite of everything the rider may essay to the contrary. Again he may be a fool and rush upon the buffaloe himself.—Hereupon the buffaloe, if he be a true old Bull, will dash his horns into the smart steed and cause no little dismay to the greenhorn rider. Horses also, that are unused to the practice, will, at the discharge of the pistol or gun, leave their master by a sudden toss alone on the plain to combat with his foe, and then O Greenhorn let thy heels be made of feathers and let thy tracks be countless. For an old Bull, has no very amiable & friendly physiognomy, when he feels 3 or 4 bullets within his rough hide.

These animals have terrible encounters with each other, and throw up the sod and dirt in splendid style; their horns are generally worn at the extremities with much fighting, and I have seen some with portions of their entrails protuding from their belly, where they have been ripped by their antagonists.

Thus did we travel on, through prairies black & brown with fat buffaloe—crossing & recrossing creeks & ravines & mounting & descending steep hills or abrupt buttes. We built a species of bridge or platform across the miry bed of the Pawnee Fork & by main strength assisted our waggons to the opposite bank.

We were destined, nevertheless to pass through this country, not without suffering some inconvenience, and like its own action, the sooner the relation of it is over, the better.

Two Chasseurs of the Company, La Jeunesse[7] and Archam-

[7] Basil Lajeunesse accompanied Frémont on both of his previous expeditions and remained with him on this trip to the West Coast. Later that year in California he was killed by Klamath Indians. LeRoy R. Hafen and W. J. Ghent, *Broken Hand, The Life Story of Thomas Fitzpatrick*, 70; Allan Nevins, *Frémont, The West's Greatest Adventurer*, I, 239.

beaux—being out some miles from the caravan on march,—came upon a large band of buffaloe, quietly feeding on the prairie and perfectly unsuspicious of their approach.

Feeling desirous of having some fat meat which is never out of season, with hungry travellers, and one being mounted on a mule—the other on a weary horse, they secured the ropes of their animals to a clump of grass, and with ready rifles crept towards the unsuspecting buffaloe. Before they attained shooting distance, a veteran Bull lifted his head and scanned the intruders. But supposing them merely to be a brace of wolves on a spying expedition, he resumed his feeding.—However he again mistrusted, and being the nearest one of the herd, to the objects in question, enjoyed superior advantage in sight. The conclusion at which he arrived was unfavorable to the hunters—and wheeling around his immense carcase he hobbled off at a swift pace, followed by the entire herd. The poor chasseurs were perfectly nonplussed, and what must have been their horror when they beheld the furious drove, rushing with all the violence of a hurricane, shape their course, in a direct line towards the 2 riding animals standing on the butte. On rolled the multitude,—the horse & mule were swept along with the tornado and the disheartened hunters arrived at the summit of the butte, only to behold their favorite animals with holsters,—pistols—bridles & saddles—dashed along with the furious buffaloe, the stamping of whose many hoofs sounded over the level and silent plain like the mutterings of a departing storm or the taunts of the manes of the slaughtered buffaloe. They returned to camp on foot, with downcast looks—& feeling perfectly crestfallen.[8]

Whilst travelling along this prairie, our route was marked by another incident expressive of the feelings with which all considered any dereliction of duty by one individual as a want of

[8] This episode is told at the end of Chapter XI of *The Western Journal*, after a more extended and rambling discussion of the buffalo and buffalo hunting than appears here.

proper feeling for the whole. The Company, as I have remarked was divided off into a certain number of guards—4 or 5 men at a time, relieved at 11½ by 5 more & these by the same number of others at 2 o'clock. To each of these guards was appointed a head or captain, whose duty it was to have his men out at the proper hour—to place them in proper positions around the camp —and regularly per each half-hour to make the rounds of the camp and notice the vigilance of his men. Now as we have re-marqued, it is an impardonable error against all your comrades, for you to take a nap on your guard, whilst travelling through these wild regions, as by your negligence you are very apt to expose the lives of your sleeping comrades and your own to what-ever savages there will always lurk about. On the same day, therefore, that the Canadians, who had lost their riding animals in the manner I have described, returned to camp, Mr. King our Botanist, a captain of a guard, was tried before Captain Frémont, for dereliction of duty by falling asleep on his guard during the previous night, on the accusation of one of his own guard. He was found guilty and sentenced to walk to Bent's fort several hundred miles distant, or leave the Company. Now seeing there was much danger in this latter resort he chose the former and commenced his pilgrimage á pied, this same day.[9]

I had almost forgotten to mention that Lajeunesse, one of the

---

[9] Chapter XI appeared in *The Western Journal* of September, 1853. It was not until March, 1856, Volume 15, Number 4, that "Chapter XII" appeared, with no other explanation than the legend under the title: "Continued from page 445, Vol. 10, *Western Journal*." Chapter XII concluded the installments in *The Western Journal*. It covered the remaining episodes in Chapter Five of the manuscript, expanded in the usual euphuistic manner. The first recognizable episode concerns the dereliction of the botanist King, presumably Henry King, a green hand recruited in Georgetown, D.C., where Mrs. Frémont had gone to school. Henry King proved a valuable member of the expedition and became commissary of the California Battalion. He was also on Frémont's Fourth Expedition. The only additional light thrown on King's lapse in *The Western Journal* is that King was lulled to sleep by the howls of a "little wolf or cayote" and that when his gun fell from his grasp, it was seized by "a cunning Frenchman who had remained awake for the very purpose." Montaignes indignantly condemns both the sentence and the Frenchman who brought the charges.

Chasseurs above mentioned, accompanied by Rouchon,[10] had mounted fresh animals and gone in search of the recreant animals who had strayed in the manner which I have narrated. They were gone during the night following the condemnation of King and the greater portion of the next day.—We therefore travelled but a short day's journey and awaited them at a place where a small rivulet flowed or rather stood in a direction East and West. Here, during the night, was our camp alarmed by the yells and fire-arms of Indians.—The men turned out, but the savages were off and nothing could be seen, the following morning, but the moccasin prints on the soil. They were supposed to be a band of wandering Pawnees as we were now travelling through the country over which that people rove, but there is good reason to believe that they were Arapahoes, as we came across a party of them, a few days after on the banks of the Smoky Hill Fork. We were someways anxious respecting the two absent men, and Captain Frémont, taking with him 3 or 4 of his men, mounted their horses and set out in search of them. They retraced the route we had travelled after they left us and striking off upon the prairie beheld them at a distance coming towards them.

When the 2 poor fellows, who had camped out all night, without having any fire or anything to eat, discovered the party riding swiftly toward them, they believed them to be Indians, and dismounting from their horses, they made ready to defend themselves. They were consequently much gratified to discover upon closer examination, that the supposed Indians, were friends in search of them and came to camp in very joyful mood. Yet at the return of this troop into camp there was a greater confusion occasioned there, for the Commander pro tem. (Dr. McDowell)[11]

---

[10] Zephyr Rouchon, a stonecutter by trade, returned from Bent's Fort under Abert's command and accepted employment at Fort Gibson. See Chapter Eighteen.

[11] *The Western Journal* says the command was left in the hands of the surgeon of the expedition but does not name him. Dr. James McDowell was a nephew of Mrs. Frémont, says Nevins, *Frémont*, 207. William Brandon, *The Men and the Moun-*

shouted aloud to drive in the mules, for the Indians were coming. All was hustle and confusion; Some were driving up the stubborn mules, some were loading their guns, and some were running here and there.

The pseudo-Indians of course rode unmolested into the camp.[12]

There exists no timber on these plains, save now & then there will be a few trees along the banks of the scanty water courses. These are generally cottonwood. There exists no other species of vegetation except the short buffaloe grass, forever kept low by the sharp molars of the grazing bands of buffaloe. We had therefore as a substitute for fire wood, to make use of that species of timber, which has been so queerly denominated by Frémont in his exceeding politeness—boisde vache and after our men became used to this, there were no great objections raised against the practice of cooking with a fire of these prairie chips.

About the 22nd or 23rd of July, we reached the uneven and bleached slopes and hills, seamed by many a rain and temporary torrent, into deep chasms and valleys, which characterize the approach to Smoky Hill Fork, of the Kanzas River. Ascending the eminences, we beheld its valley stretching North East and Southwest, covered with a somewhat greener carpeting than the surface of the neighboring hills,—whilst the broad channel filled with

---

tain, 91, lists him as her cousin. Frémont, *Memoirs,* 427, says that because McDowell wanted to return home before winter, he accompanied Abert's party from Bent's Fort. Abert, however, does not list McDowell as a member of his command or mention him in his report.

[12] This incident, related by Frémont in his *Memoirs,* is one of two instances in which Frémont verifies details given in Montaignes' journal. Frémont, however, says Lajeunesse and Rouchon were looking for an animal that had strayed during the night. He does not mention the horse and mule stampeded by buffalo. Frémont agrees with Montaignes that the staged Indian raid furnished ample proof that the men in camp were ill prepared for an emergency. "It was midday," he writes, "and the people were careless and more occupied by getting the dinner than with Indians. . . . Our charge gave them a good lesson, though it lasted but a moment. It was like charging into a beehive; there were so many men in the camp ready with their rifles that it was very unsafe to keep up our Indian character beyond the moment of the charge. Still, like all excitements, it stirred the blood pleasantly for the moment." *Ibid.,* II, 425–26,

muddy and thick water, wound away among the hills like some enormous tape-line.

We approached its edge and encamped on the sand, of which its banks are composed.

CHAPTER SIX

Wherein new dramatis personae are introduced upon the stage with marvellous effect, and the Curtain remains hoisted untill the 1st of August.

THE Smoky hill fork of Caw River.—huge masses of clay or slate.—appearance of the water of this fork.—a Band of Arapahoes or Rapahoes.—Their demeanour and designs.—their chief—their approach,—their village, 4 day's travel distant.—They kill buffaloe for us.—They leave us the 2nd day.—The queer headpiece of a certain old one among them. The 26th of July—Cheyennes—3 or 4 hundred.— their village—droves of mules and horses.—Encamp one mile from the tent—Squaws—Children—warriors and dogs,—larettes, moccasins—buffaloe meat etc.—our departure.—hair ropes—We camp on Smokey—very little water in the channel.— The 27th—the 28th—The 29th—Dry Fork—30th Camp without water—Arkansas river in the distance.—magnanimous act of Capt. Frémont narrated. 31st. Pond of water—strike the Spanish Trace again—Bent's fort 20 miles distant.—Encamp on the Arkansas.—1st of August.

Smokey Hill Branch is one of the principal tributaries of the

Kanzas River, and after flowing in almost a due Eastern direction for about 550 or 600 miles it empties into that river about 200 miles above its deboucement into the Missouri. It derives its name doubtless from the dusky & sombre scenery through which it flows, and its water is of a dusky and smoky colour being well impregnated with clay & sand. So thick indeed was the water with these materials that it could not be used for culinary purposes untill allowed to settle. The banks, at this point where we struck it, were composed of a white species of plaster[1] or soft clay and white sand, being so extremely undurable as to be ploughed into deep furrows by every descending rain. A few old Bulls were noticed by us among the chasm of this portion, appearing not unlike the shades of fabled leviathans wandering among the ruins of ancient cities.

We followed the course of this stream towards the West for several days, passing over table plains spotted with buffaloe, and dotted now & then by flocks of timid antelope. We came across several tolerable springs of water now & then, but for the most part, we viewed a rise of the water of the River which seemed to become purer as we approached its sources. Still we saw no Indians. Several times did we notice black specks along the distant edges of the horizon,—but from the proximity to buffaloe, we judged them to be bulls rather than Indians spying our movements.

Thus did we journey on, now following the banks of the Fork, —now & then crossing its shallow channel—and mounting the hills on the other side and pursuing our track over the level prairie, without coming in contact with any of the savage dwellers of the region, & without having our monotonous travel interspersed with any other episodes save the killing of an antelope or buffaloe.

Finally on the 24th of July, as we left our Camp which we had

[1] Gypsum.

52

pitched in a little vale,—and ascended the heigths which conducted to the edges of the main prairie, a quick shout from some
keen eyed comrade drew the attention of the caravan, to a group of
wild forms on horseback, gallopping out into view from the concealment of a distant hill on the opposite side of the river.
They were several miles distant, yet their dusky forms and dark
coloured horses—were plainly discernible, though the back
ground of the phantasgamora was nought but the sombre sides of
the sandhills well deserving the title of Smokey; one 2.3.4.5.6
rode into view and reined up their steeds as if to enjoy a good
view of our band as it moved over the plains,—in bold relief
between them and the bright sky.—1.2.3.4 5 & 6 more soon
joined them,—then a group more & so on untill there was a complete crowd of horsemen. We did not halt however, and though
their appearance caused some little surprise, it did not deter our
travel. They wished to treat with us, it appeared, for one of them
dismounted, & holding up a blanket to our view,—spread it
smoothly upon the ground, thereby expressing his and his companions' desire no doubt to have an amicable understanding with
us. Even this did not change our course or in the least lessen the
pace at which we were then moving, and they, coming to a second
resolution, in a moment, struck their heels into their steeds sides
and commenced fording the River, one following the other, in
order to come up to us.

Hereupon, our Caravan came to a halt. Our waggons were
driven into the form of a circle, which manoeuvre is designated
by the Spaniards as a carál, into which we drove all our loose
mules and pack animals.

Dismounting we secured our riding animals to the waggons—
and ammunition being distributed all hands stood around the
edge of the circle or carál with ready gun, to await the foe.

The Indians had now crossed the river, & came into sight one
after the other, as they gallopped their fleet steeds towards us over

the plain. The Chief came forwards first, having upon his head a great war cap of bright feathers and beads. He rode up to our leader and shook hands in most friendly style. The balance of the band about 30 odd, followed, & by their amicable demeanour removed all apprehensions on our part of a rupture. Our caravan got under weigh again, and our new friends having been out only on a Pawnee hunt, they now changed their course and accompanied us that day, as we were going in the direction of their village which was 4 days' travel distant, or about 100 miles.

They were a grim looking set, and with their curious queus covered with plates of silver,—their leggings mocassins with long fringes,—their long and murderous looking lances,—their bows and arrow their snowwhite shields of buffaloe hide and their smart little steeds, with long manes & tails, as wild as themselves, snorting & snuffing in the morning breeze, they were altogether a barbarous & fantastic group, & answered exactly to all the ideas I had previously formed of the appearance of a warparty of wild prairie Indians. Their first desire was for Tobacco, and it is curious how the love of this leaf has reached these roving tribes with so much strength as it has. They were willing to trade almost anything they had for it, and the men, with such currency managed to supply themselves with several pairs of moccasins.

These Indians camped with us the night of the 24th and did not leave us untill the next day, at evening. However, before parting with us, they discovered that buffaloe meat was in demand among us, and that Tobacco might be obtained in return for some, and being assured of this by our Captain, they handed their shields and other dispensables, to the white horsemen to carry for them, & sped away on their wild horses in pursuit of buffaloe.—They killed several, and being well rewarded for the meat thereof they spent the greater part of the day in this amusement, so that before the Araphoes left us to go to their village, our waggons were again laden with a plentiful supply of rich beef.

We nooned on the 25th at a small branch—flowing into the Smokey—and before night-fall had moved on some 6 or 8 miles farther and encamped on a refreshing little stream of flowing water, where we build comfortable fires & jerked our meat.

The following morning (The 26th). we made an early start from this pleasant little camping place,—leaving several old Bulls near by, to speculate on the sights they saw, and crossing the little stream in question, moved across the prairie at the rate of about 3 miles an hour. We had not proceeded more than 6 or 7 miles—before an Indian on horseback was seen on the edge of the horizon before us, another, was soon joined to the first and before half an hour.—there were 3 or 4 hundred Cheyennes on horseback advancing towards us at a gallop from over the hill.[2] They come in groups of 6–8 or ten,—and gallop in a circle around us.—We form a carál,—dismount and make ready for battle. Our Pilot and interpreter rides forth to meet them.—they ride up to us—shake hands and so forth. Afar off we hear the singing of many men, & behold 30 or 40 warriors riding abreast and singing in a low but harmonious voice—approach us.

They are friendly and mix with us like brothers. We break up the carál and march to their village which is just beyond the next butte.

We encamp within a mile of the Indian town whose brown and white tents are placed in a large circle, and find one large one in the centre which belongs to the medicine, and the inhabitants warriors—squaws—children & dogs sally out to greet and to see us. A Grand meeting is held in the Captain's tent with the

---

2 Frémont, *Memoirs*, II, 425, corroborates Montaignes' account: "On the high plains we encountered a Cheyenne village which was out on a hunt. The men came to meet us on the plain, riding abreast and their drums sounding. They were in all their bravery, and the formidable line was imposing, and looked threatening to those of our people who were without experience in an Indian country . . . . But the Cheyennes were friendly, and we on our side were too strong for any exhibition of hostility or rudeness; and so we gave the usual present in exchange for friendly conduct and good wishes."

chiefs of the tribe—respecting a trade for meat, larettes[3] and moccasins, and in a short time, the camp presents all the appearance of a camp of traders.—Indians of both sexes bringing in buffaloe ropes,—robes—moccasins etc.—and now and then an old squaw bending beneath the weight of a parflêche of meat.— young braves with leggings covered with bright beads—and old ones sitting in groups smoking pipes of kin-ne-kin-nik.

By 1 o'clock, the trading was pretty much over,—and as the Indians began to draw off towards their village with their acquisitions of beads—knives—mirrors and tobacco, we caught up our animals.—packed our mules & started. As we ascended an eminence, which overlooked the Indian camp, we were enabled to see the town to advantage, and all its surrounding droves of horses & mules feeding among the hills. Every now and then, a little brave, not larger than a radish would scour past us on horseback, with all the pride and vanity and dignity of a Cheyenne, whilst several old coons accompanied us during an hour's travel.

We camped on Smokey Fork this night; with several of our new friends as guests:

Among other inventions among these people is that of ropes made from the long hair of buffaloe—as likewise frequently from horsehair.

The next morning being the 27th, we started at 5½ o'clock and travelled till 12. Very scarce water at this place.

28th Started at ½ past 5, and travelled over a hot and barren

---

[3] Larette or lazo—called by the Canadians Cabresse [word illegible] of rope, manufactured from buffaloe hide, which is cut into slips or strings of equal length and plaited, 3 double sometimes 4. They are very strong and of different lengths; according to the taste of the maker. The Mexicans secure an Iron Ring to one end and make a noose out of it, with which they catch mules & horses. Hastings in his Journal has mentioned that the Californians catch even bear by its means.— Montaignes' note. [Lansford W. Hastings, *The Emigrants Guide to Oregon and California*, 1845. A lawyer from Mount Vernon, Ohio, he led overland expeditions and is notorious as discoverer of the Hastings Cut-Off, which some emigrant parties followed, much to their sorrow.]

plain with very little water, & but few antelope to be seen. Some few wild horses and buffaloe were seen.—Tonight we encamp on Smokey Hill Fork for the last time. The water was barely flowing. —Rain this night. The next day, the 29th, we encamped on Dry Fork.—20 miles distant. no water save that which seeped through the sand. At this place, the individuals of one of the messes judging from the increasing aridity of the region, that we would have soon to camp without water, used the precaution to fill a keg and place it in their waggon for such an extremity.

Therefore crossing this Dry Fork, which so well merits its title, we proceeded across a warm and barren country till nearly sundown. Orders were given to halt and though there was no water closer than the Arkansas which was seen by some stragglers in the distant view, we turned our animals loose and sat down to a supper of Indian jerked beef.

This was dry and hard, and but caused us to feel the want of water more severly. Here then were the members of the 2nd mess, to enjoy the benefits of their foresighted prudence and luxuriate on a supper of warm coffee and cooked meat. But alas how often are men deceived. Their fire of prairie chips was hardly underweigh, when the sable valet-de-cham[bre] Mesty-Wollah appeared and demanded the keg of water, for the use of his master and himself.

The keg was surrendered and the fire was extinguished, whilst the fire burnt splendid at the tent of the Captain and fragrant odours as of boiling coffee greeted the nasal organs of the thirsty camp, proceeding from the coffeepot which simmered for the Captain's own use. This was the 30th.

This night the exhausted beeves which had been driven thus far, and were scarcely able to walk they were so poor & famished, had new strength given them by extraordinary thirst, and rushed beyond the power of the guards, and ran about the prairie looking for water.

Long ere the sun of the 31st was above the East—our caravan
was several miles distant from this Thirsty Camp and we cheered
ourselves with the hope of arriving before sundown at some pond
or hole of water, wherewith to allay our thirst.

We had not to travel all day however, for ere the sun had
arrived at the centre of his daily course, we perceived several
miles in advance of us, a thin smoke arising from the plain, and
our leader & pilot there before us. We hailed the sign with pleasure and we travelled forward with renewed vigor. Our poor
mules whom we were forced to charge about every hour or so, soon
pricked up their ears & seemed to share the general excitement.

They moved on faster & faster untill their pace turned into a
swift run, so that the drivers could scarcely retain them, and in
one grand meleé the waggons—drivers—mules—horses—riders
—& pack mules moved over the prairie like a terrified band of
buffaloe towards the pond.

The mules without waiting to be eased of their packs rushed
into the water & drank almost to bursting. The men stooped down
to the water's edge and drank and drank again—whilst many
made drinking cups of their hats and swallowed from them many
a goodly draught. We remained here to rest untill about 12
o'clock. All hands then packed up and struck out for the Spanish
trail[4] which we reached about 8 miles distant.

That night we encamped on the Arkansas about 25 miles distant
from Bent's Fort.

[4] This Trail or Road is not the one which traders generally follow in journeying
to Santa Fé, for it crosses the Arkansas many miles below Bent's Fort. But it is the
one the only one which waggons from this post, travel, to reach the settlements.—
Montaignes' note.

CHAPTER SEVEN

The incidents related in this chapter occupy the space of 10 days, at the expiration of which time we shall not be 10 hours journey from the place where we be at present.

AN Indian grave—Mexico on the other side of the River.—Arrival at the Fort.—The Delawares.—herds of horses and Cattle.—Our Salute.—Mejicanos—French, and half-breeds.—Our Camp.—a mule dies.—The beeves—Mexican mule drivers from Taos.—The Dragoons.—The horsemanship of the Mexicans.—The one armed Español.—The approach of our old friends—the Chienne nation.—Their old [w]omen and their dogs.—The Chiennes have a council with the Delawares.—They rejoice because they have taken a Pawnee Scalp.—the appearance of their braves.—their music.—The Songs of the Delawares.—Preparations in Camp for a departure.—the mules shod.—A Cheyenne dance.—their music—their reward by our Captain.—The events of 5 o'clock P.M. on the 10th of August.—Orders issued for the Camanche Company to cross the Arkansas.—7 o'clock.—all arrayed. Fitzpatrick.—pickets—raincoats etc. Rain.

The first day of August arrived, and the sun arose warm and invigorating, apparently to cheer us for the hard times we had experienced, and we journied on our way, along the North bank of the river, with joyful hearts, expecting to see each minute, the turrets of the far famed fort Bent on the horizon.

As we thus travelled along we could not but notice what a sterile and untillable region this was,—and could not but speculate to

59

ourselves how many thousand years would yet roll over, ere men would be forced by their multitude to seek a livelihood by plough-ing its bosom, and sewing seeds among its rock and gravel. Again we thought to ourselves what would be the fate of those roving savages who roam over its wastes and live by pursuing the buffaloe and robbing the passers by? Alas, considered we to our-selves as the remembrance of slaughtered buffaloe returned, when these herds are gone the red men of these plains shall either leave this soil or die upon its wastes. Just then we lifted our eyes to the scene around us, & we beheld a something swung aloft in a decayed tree bearing some resemblance to a suspended canoe. Twas the grave of an Indian. "Ah" muttered we in heart, as the spectacle struck our gaze. "If all your dead require a tree to perch upon, the better to behold the path which leads to the Happy hunting grounds, then there is little hope for the most of ye!"

Indeed the aspect of the surrounding country was sterile enough, to be sure, and save along the banks of the Arkansas, not a tree was to be discerned. Even these were being thinned for the purpose of fuel to supply the fort and we encamped at a place where there was nought but small willows and whatever scanty drift wood was cast ashore by the annual freshets.

Here we remained for a couple of hours to prepare for our triumphal Entry.—The American stars and stripes were hoisted on the little carriage,—each man dressed out in his best,—and when the order to "Catch up & Saddle" was given,—the men went at it like new and fresh hands. 6 or 7 Delaware Indians joined us at this place.—They had reached the Fort in advance of us, and having waited there for several days, had now come out to meet us. They were mostly good looking fellows & the very beauideal of dashing braves. We arrived at the fort about 3 o'clock PM and advancing with our little army up to its very walls, we saluted the inmates with several hundred discharges from our arms. They answered us with a shot from their cannon—and we camped within a mile on the river.

Whilst encamped at this place we had many opportunities of visiting this fort, and of noting the class of people, by whom the various offices are carried on.—I shall not detain the reader with more trifles than possible, but I shall essay to afford him some slight idea of what a mountain trading post is, by the rough description which I shall give of this.

Fort William or Bent's Fort stands on the north bank of the Arkansas river about 1000 miles from its mouth. It is a post of many years standing and its proprietors carry on a brisk trade with the surrounding tribes and annually import, by means of waggons, great quantities of furs and robes, into the American settlements of Missouri. Immediately opposite, on the other side of the Arkansas is the region called North Mexico,—and about 180 miles, in a direction almost south is Santa Fé, to which Dorado of Traders there is a trail passing this fort. Taos (pronounced Tause) is another Mexican town about 90 miles distant, from which place the fort is supplied with flour and corn. Pike's peak is plainly discernible from Bent's Post, and the mongrel town of Pueblo, which is said to be at the foot of the main chain of mountains is 70 odd miles off. The country at which this fort is built is unfortunately nearly destitute if not entirely, of rock suitable for building, and the architects who formed the walls, have had recourse to that plan invented and so much followed by the people of Mexico viz: To make their walls of sun-dried brick called adobes. These when well laid form a firmer wall than might be expected, and after they have remained beneath the burning rays of the sun for some time, they can withstand many peltings of wind and rain, ere they become soft.

Such is the material of which Bent's fort like all those in similar positions, is composed, though the ordinary woodwork, such as

beams—rafters—posts etc is executed the same as in other buildings. The entire concern, is in the form of a quadrangle: Two
bastions at opposite corners,—a yard for cattle towards the West
side,—whilst all around in the interior are various rooms—stores
—shops—and so forth—built out [of] adobes like the main wall.
A watch tower stands upon the roof over the gate which opens on
the East, and a press for baling robes ornaments the centre of the
area or yard.

There are usually 2 or more of the partners at the place at
once to see that things are going on right, whilst the interior is
generally filled with a complement of clerks—traders—engagés
—cooks,—Spaniards—team drivers—hired hunters & free trappers. At the season of the year at which we arrived here, the place
was comparatively empty. T'was no season for trappers,—The
waggons we had met, on their route towards the settlements, and
neither was it the season for Indian trading. It was built I suppose,
more with the purpose of being a place of security against the
treachery of Savages than a place of importance in the eyes of
any nation. No matter what it was; we nevertheless rode up, to
its gates, and with our stars & stripes floating in the breeze saluted
it with about 300 charges of powder. They answered us with their
cannon and the welkin rang.

A motley group of half-breeds—whole breeds etc issued from
the gates, and this was our arrival at Bent's Fort.[1]

We pitched our camp, on the river bank, about one mile below,
thanking God in our hearts that at least we were here without
accident of any note, and wishing at the bottom of our heart that
we were safe and sound at the place from which we started.

At this place, as had been anticipated, our leader, immediately

[1] Bent's Old Fort on the Arkansas (Otero County, Colorado, eight miles north-
east of La Junta) was opened as a fur-trading post in 1833 by Charles and William
Bent and became important as a way station on the Santa Fe Trail. It was abandoned
in 1849. David Lavender, *Bent's Fort*; George Bird Grinnell, "Bent's Old Fort and
Its Builders," *Kansas Historical Society Collections*, Vol. XV (1919–22).

commenced preparations for a division of the Company, as he
had orders, in order that one portion under the command of
himself should cross the mountains and proceed towards California, whilst the other under the nominal command of Lieutenant Abert,[2] but under the pilotage & management of Mister Fitzpatrick[3] the mountaineer, should cross the Ratone Spurs and
following the Spanish Trace untill near Taos, then strike off East
& return to the settlements of the United States by way of Texas
and the south fork of the Canadian, called by the Spaniards, the
Colorado or Red River. This division, however, was not to be
made in a day, and we remained encamped at this place 9 days,
ere the south company crossed the River as a preparatory step to
a grand start on their Journey Homeward. There were several
additional considerations which influenced the Captain, and besides wishing to recruit his animals, which were become quite

[2] Abert's report of that phase of the expedition described in the following chapters
of Montaignes' journal is printed with a map as 29th Cong., 1 sess., *Sen. Doc. 438*, Vol.
VIII (1846), under the title *Journal of Lieutenant Abert from Bent's Fort to St. Louis
in 1845*. See also *Guádal P'a*. Frémont, *Memoirs*, 426, commends the two lieutenants:
"It is well to say here that on the journey to Bent's Fort I had been much prepossessed
in their favor. They had shown themselves well qualified for such an expedition
which as [*sic*] of course was entirely new to them. In this journey they had given
evidence of the prudence and good judgment which enabled them to carry through
successfully the expedition entrusted to their care." His wife Jessie, however, had
faint praise in writing to Professor John Torrey of West Point: "Young Abert's
report accompanies this—perhaps it may be of some interest, although he seems
unskilled in exploration." Quoted in Goetzmann, *Army Exploration*, 123. No one
seems to have remarked that Frémont rid himself of both lieutenants—one of them
the son of his commanding officer—before embarking on his filibuster to California.

[3] Thomas Fitzpatrick, one of the most famous of the Mountain Men, awaited the
Frémont expedition at Bent's Fort after guiding Colonel Stephen Watts Kearny and
the 1st Dragoons to South Pass. Fitzpatrick, born in County Cavan, Ireland, in 1799,
accompanied General William Henry Ashley up the Missouri in the famous expedition of 1823. He was with Jedediah Smith in the small party that made the effective
discovery of South Pass in 1824. In 1830 Fitzpatrick became partner in the Rocky
Mountain Fur Company but quit the fur trade in 1840. He guided the party that
included Father Pierre De Smet and John Bidwell in 1841, and in 1843, he led
the second Frémont expedition. After guiding Abert in 1845, Fitzpatrick accompanied Kearny on his Mexican War campaign of 1846, returning from Socorro to
Washington with dispatches. In 1847 he began a notable career as Indian agent. He
died in Washington in 1854. Hafen and Ghent, *Broken Hand*; Hiram M. Chittenden,
The American Fur Trade of the Far West.

lean with travelling, he hoped to exchange several of them, for fresh ones, and obtain supplies of provisions. It was his expectation to procure flour, rice—sugar—coffee etc. which had been left for the use of the men under his command, but which to our dismay, was nearly all taken by the party of dragoons who had returned by this route,—from escorting a caravan of Oregon emigrants through the Indian country. One of our mules died whilst here & was thrown into the Arkansas.—The Cheyenne nation also,—our old friends of smoky Hill fork, desirous of keeping up an intimacy with us were beheld in full motion, approaching the fort, a few days after our arrival, with all their lodges,—squaws—children,—dogs—& droves of horses.—They advanced in long phalanxes—beating their barbarous drums, and singing in a most terrific style. They drummed and marched around awhile & pitched their village of tents and lodges—between us and the Fort. Their squaws rode upon mules their dogs dragged tent poles after them & frequently a mule would canter past with an old man secured on a frame in the Rear.

For 2 nights was their barbarous music continually ajar,— They had taken a Pawnee Scalp and they were greatly rejoiced. I do believe that if these savages were to take one scalp & lose 20, they would think themselves fortunate & beat their drums & have a dance.[4]

The Shians however had another design in coming to us, for some time ago, their braves had slain several Delaware warriors, amongst the balance the Delaware war-chief, whose son was among the men who accompanied us. T'was therefore the desire of both parties to hold a powow and make some species of peace treaty for the murder aforesaid.[5] In the mean time, these Indians

[4] The Cheyenne scalp dance is described in detail by George Bird Grinnell, *The Cheyenne Indians*, II, 39–44.

[5] Lieutenant Abert says all the Indians sat on the floor with their backs straight against the wall of the chief's tent. After the discussion, they smoked the peace pipe.

crowded our camp and roamed around at leisure to examine the strange things of the white men.

The general appearance of these Indians is far better than that of most of the prairie Indians, and I have seen some very good looking men among them, though none are renowned for beauty. The young braves play the beaux to satisfaction and they strutted about our camp—with their red faces shining with grease,— their long queus well ornamented with silver plates of various sizes almost trailing upon the ground—and their beaded leggings & moccasins, with an air of great importance,—as much as to say, "See here white face, how a Cheyenne can look." They also must needs favour us with a dance, and after their young girls had tripped it at the fort on their light elastic toes, for the amusement of the inmates thereof,—the young braves thought it but discreet that we should not be forgotten, and thereupon gathered together their drums and rattles, and under the guidance of a chief musician and a master of ceremonies who held a spear, & was mounted on a horse bedaubed with yellow clay, and danced a reel at our Captain's tent which some said, was the "prairie wolf dance." There were 6 or 8 dancers, I believe, and these were ornamented in divers ways, both with paint & mud & feathers and beads. They jumped up & down with bent knees, shaking little rattles and bells: Whilst the fellows with painted faces—were beating drums made of stretched Buffaloe hide and singing in a doleful voice. The Chief musician, an old sinful looking devil, commenced the tune by giving a slight stroke with his drumstick upon his tomtom and uttering a slight groan,—the balance would follow, increasing the violence of their stroke and their humming and groaning,

---

The Indian passing the pipe handed it from person to person, giving it to each in a particular manner. To one, for example, he turned the stem toward the ground. To another he handed the bowl first. Both Delawares and Cheyennes seemed to under-stand the significance of every motion, to know why each received the pipe in his particular way. Each member of the council took one long draught and handed the pipe back to the individual who passed it. *Journal*, 2.

untill their music would almost deafen you—and then lowering
their music untill you could scarcely hear it. The whole would
end with a simultaneous yell or bark from the whole group, and
a look behind to see if the beads & tobacco was yet forthcoming.
A multitude of the tribe was also present to view the glorious
debut of their young braves, and it would have made you, feel
quite risible to notice the good hearted old squaws, who would
every now and then join in the song with their shrill voices with
as much pleasure and gratification as if they made all the music
themselves. At the termination of the dances for there were a
series of them (those Cheyennes or Shians would be clever hands
at a reel) tobacco, knives, little looking glasses etc, were brought
out and divided among them for their trouble and these savages
appeared much pleased.

About 5 o'clock on the evening of the tenth: orders were issued
for all those whose names were for the South Company, to take
up their plunder & cross to the opposite side of the river.

The Chienne Dance.

at Bent's Fort

The horses & mules for each Company were already selected
—Mr. Fitzpatrick our intended pilot was arrived,—the provisions were likewise divided—Each man knew his destination, and
we therefore, each took possession of an animal & forded the
river. Here we pitched our tents, and this was the 1st camp of the
Famous Piquetwah,—Ratone—Big Bear—anti Frémont—Texian and Cutnose Expedition, whose adventures good and bad, &
whose awful dangers and difficulties, in their passage from Bent's
fort through the Great American Desart, shall form the material
which composes the following pages.

CHAPTER EIGHT

*Which describes the incidents which took place at Bent's fort,
whilst the famous and glorious Piquitwah—Ratone—Big Bear
—anti Frémont—Cutnose and Camanche Expedition was encamped near that place—as also certain remarks touching the
officers—appearance and members of the said Expedition.*

BEFORE transporting my read-
ers and myself, to any inconvenient distance from this place,
yclept Bent's Fort, I shall take the opportunity of throwing in a
few remarks which although not strictly within the compass
usually allowed for the orbit of a Journalizer, are nevertheless
not irrelavant to the subject, and are such as are naturally brought
on by the association of things.

The trading posts or forts, so called locally, are the hearts, to
use a figure, through which the entire commerce of these western
regions seeks a channel into distant countries. They engross, as it

were all the trade both of mountains & prairie, & then by a second operation, spread it far & wide through far off lands.

The numerous traders, hunters trappers etc, which constitute the instruments by which the said action is carried on, form a feature of humanity, at once wild and roving, but, whose vocation is at the same time often invested with such a charm of novelty and apparent independence, as to catch the eye of the enlightened passenger, and at once transform him into a leather clad rover of the desert. Consequently, in a class of this order, wherein, one would scarce expect to find a mind enlightened and a disposition of greatness, there are, and have been, numerous individuals, who though clothed in savage attire, and hideous selon la coutume des montaignes, have minds endowed with knowledge concealed beneath a wool cap, and a heart beating with every feeling of honour, and greatness confined by the coarse shirt and the buckskin hunting shirt. There are many, I say, of this order, yet, and I am loth to say so, the characteri[sti]c general feature of the trader and hunter & trapper of the mountains and the plains, is that of mean—base cunning and selfishness,—a heart full of treachery,—thoughts and promises made of wind, and no mind at all.

The trapper is usually qualified for his profession by a long and patient apprenticeship,—and a series of dangerous and frequently fatal ordeals, of privation, suffering,—guarding, watching, winds & storms and Indian encounters.

So that, by the time he devotes several years to the profession, and 'scape free from Indians & death, he becomes a trapper, and depending upon his courage and success, the traders who control the trade, engage his services, and send him forth to entrap the furbearing animals for their benefit.

If he feel himself capable of acting independently of the traders, he set up business as the saying is, on his own account, and he hunts and traps, (for these professions are seldom separate) for himself, and disposes of the proceeds of his labour to the merchants, in return for whatever he be necessitated to have in order to carry on his business. He is what may be and is termed a "Free Trapper."

The Indians however who live by hunting and trapping,—are jealous of the whitemen, take advantage of every opportunity which is afforded and frequently fall upon the wandering trapper or trappers, and making [away] with the owners, appropriate the proceeds of their labour, to their own exclusive benefit.

In such onslaughts however the ever wary & courageous mountaineer, is so often found by his enemies, prepared and bold hearted, & ready to defend his property and life untill death, that the acquisition of a white man's scalp is considered by them a victory worthy of a triumph equal to Alexander's or Caesor's.

Again—as the animals, whose fur is sought for by the trapper, and eagerly trafficked for by the merchant, gradually decreases in number & will finally totally disappear, so will the profession of trapper naturally become less profitable untill at length, the trappers will also disappear and nought but the famous deeds of daring and danger, of former individuals, will form the history of the profession and professors.

Of men of this class and of such Mexicans as chance or business brought to the place, was the inhabitants of Bent's Fort composed, together with clerks, traders and herdsmen whose business it was to drive the horses, mules and cattle out some distance from the Fort, and then keep them in good pasture ground untill night & then drive them up to the Fort again.

The cattle are Spanish or Mexican cattle and are generally fine beeves. The horses are mostly Indian and Spanish, very few American, whilst the mules are entirely Spanish.

Whilst at this fort I had the opportunity afforded me, though I did not take advantage of it, and consequently describe but from report, of beholding a feat of horsemanship which would have elicited a huzzah from a Roman amphitrion[1] or obtained the praise of a Scythian rider.

T'was nothing more nor less than the mounting and breaking (as is the expression) of a wild horse, or to speak more definitely of a horse which had never felt the weight of a rider upon his back.

The circumstances relating to this preformance I shall relate, in the words of one who saw it, & shall recommend the passing reader to notice the description, as it is not only true, but it illustrates well, as by an example, the daring and seldom unsuccessful Equestrianism, for which it is proverbial that the Northern Mexicans are so famous.

The Camanches themselves cannot excel them.

The Wild Horse Tamed[2]

"Well now If ye're going to hear, why hear; becase as ye see I want's to be ater crossin this darned arkansas again and git to camp. Ye see I went up to the Fort, along with Bill and Jim, and jes as we got thar, thar were a crowd of our fellers and the Fort fellers standin outside the gate.

We thort as how we mout as well see too, what war goin on inside the crowd, and of all the dancin, & snortin, ever I heard t'was that cussed hoss's who was inside o'that crowd. He war foaming & plungin 'round as if he war dangerous & wanted to play deuce with some o'us, and I know if a thousand silver big round bright new dollars war offered to me down on the spot I wouldn't have mounted on that hoss's back. He war however a derned good looking feller and his head & eyes war some;! I tell you. His mane and tail too,—how fine they was! and cleaned

---

[1] The word appears to be "amphitrion," although Amphitryon was neither Roman nor equestrian. Montaignes may have intended the Greek Amphistratus, mythological charioteer of Castor and Pollux, or the Roman Ascanius, the young horseman of Vergil's *Aeneid*.

[2] An early (1845) description of bronco breaking as well as an early attempt to reproduce the dialect of the Mountain Man.

limbed at that and as slick as a plate of Linseed Ile. He war altogether a few. I guess as how them darned black looking devil ye calls Spaniels, thort he were muchos.

They got a bridle with a spanish bit, and after a bit of a scrimmage as an Irishman would say they got it fitted to his head. And then several held him, whilst a great lousy black whiskered fellow called Pedrow mounted up on to the horses back, & was tied on. Yes, Tied on, and lashed tight too, as if he war a mule pack and war about to start. He had a great, pair of spurs with pints, as long as my thumb and what did the darned feller do as soon, as they let go the bridle & rope, but scrape his heels up and down again the hoss'es sides, as if he war goin to rake off the hide. I do believe that o'what he was ater. and the hoss thought so too, I'll bet a quarter, for he judged by the lousy Spaniel's looks before he got on, that he wanted to gouge him.

So the horse, as soon as Pedrow, got on top o' him commenced rearing & plunging and a dartin & snortin & kickin up in the air, in such a way as ought to have teetolly demolished half a baker's dozen Pedrows. But Pedrow stuck too tight for him, and he kept raking his heels along the hoss's side fit to kill. The hoss as I said, at first tried to dash Pedrow over his head, but this wouldn't take, so he reared up & tried to pitch him off behind, but that wouldn't do nuther. So he jumped first this side then tother to git him off on one side, but it was all no go, so he thought he would jist try what vartue thar war in pure straight-forward runnin & he sets off with Pedrow like a tornado or a pig with his head in a punkin. The last we saw of Pedrow he war flying over the prairie about 3 mile off.

Now I tell you that hoss war some, and That Spaniole war some too—for If he didn't stick that horseback like a leech or a fly-plaster my name isnt Tom Davis."

To conclude this description of our friend, we shall inform the reader, that the Spanish Pedro continued lashed to the back of

71

the wild horse—and rode it untill it was humbled & then returned to the fort with it: perfectly docile and ready to mount.

This superior horsemanship of the Northern Mexicans is not to be wondered at, when we reflect that their employment is nought but trading in mules & horses,—in raising and tending them, and therefore compelled as it were, to pass a species of ordeal, so that at the close they become immuned to the service, become confident of their skill and dare mount the wildest.

The provinces of Northern Mexico, principally the country watered by the tributaries and main river called Del Norte, is a famous country for the raising of animals,—and the Cavejardes of this region and the Ranchos of the Lower Country produce thousands of healthy strong mules which are extensively purchased and used for many purposes by Drivers and Traders in these regions.

As to the horses which are raised in these provinces, I know nothing, but If I were to judge from the samples which I saw of them among the neighbouring tribes of Cayquas & Camanches, I would say that they are not to be compared with the American horse either in size,—beauty—or utility. However those which I saw, were clean limbed and very well proportioned: yet they are light and not fit for draught.

The Indians who infest the prairies frequently make descents upon the Mexican herds & select what they choose. Whenever an Indian becomes desirous of an animal to ride, or one for his squaw or one to trade or some for the name of the thing (For their notions of wealth, are in proportion to the number of horses & mules and papooses each one has) he collects together a band of his fellow braves—dresses for war and sets out towards the south. When in the neighborhood of a Cavejarde or drove of animals, they make an onset upon the herdsman, and with his scalp & his mules or horses, they go as they came.

It is wondrous wise in the people of these provinces, exposed as they are to the incursions of these barbarous tribes to keep a truce with them, yet truce or no truce, the latter insist upon levying upon the animals of the former, and taking as it were a sufficient bonus of scalps and horses, every now and then to preserve their names as superiors, among their would be friends. T'is vain on the other hand for the cowardly and impotent Mexicans to endeavor a retaliation, or even a pursuit, for these wild invaders seldom come down into their lands, except in war parties, and can disappear in a few hours to such a distance as to defy all pursuit. They are indeed the Bedouins of America. Their home is the desart and plain, and their houses are everywhere and can scarcely be found. Their tents are moved as if by magic and whilst you meet with & treat with the braves, their village perhaps is 200 miles distant, near some creek or spring far away upon the level plain.

To sum up the whole, such nations as the Cayquas or Kiowas and Camanches, as also the Euts and Apaches, are disagreeable neighbours & can pounce down upon the unhappy hamlets & ranchos of Mexico with the fleetness of a hailstorm; and the former not a bit the wiser.

They have also attempted to carry out the same system of warfare & plunder with the Americans of Texas and Coahuila. But here as may be naturally supposed, they find their match, and the Massacre at San Antonio de Bejar, has infused a panic into the Camanches and their allies, which will make them forever shun the too intimate society of such men as Texian Americans.

Though these heathens be a wild and ignorant set, they are soon taught, who they cannot trifle with and in this, they are quick scholars.

They profess great friendship for Americans and extraordinary hatred towards Texians. But when they discover that these same Texians are nothing else but true & Simon pure Americans,

they will easily come to the resolve, to preserve as strong a friendship for them: as Prudence is the better part of valour and at the
same time in their case, by all means the best policy. I am, however, forgetting the subject of the present chapter, and shall therefore immediately resume the description of such circumstances
as happened during our sojourn near the aforesaid Fort.

At the termination of the last chapter, I mentioned that Capt
Frémont, having announced to the men under his command, which
were to remain under his own, and which were to be hereafter
under that of Lieutenant Abert, likewise issued an additional
order to the effect, that all those whose names were set down as
belonging to the South Company under Abert, should immediately cross the Arkansas with the waggons, horses, provisions and
plunder which had already been apportioned out to them. It will
not be considered as a mark of ungenerosity in me, if I here
remark, that the characteristic· quality of the said, horses and
mules, given to us by Captain Frémont for our peculiar benefit,
was not of the superior class, and it was with extreme regret that
we were compelled not only to give up, such iron pickets as any
of us unfortunate ones happened to have, but likewise to deliver
to the favorites of the Sublime Porte, whatever rain-coats which
were unhappily among us.

These privations were submitted to, with extraordinary forti-
tude, as we, one and all, felt ourselves amply rewarded by the
bright prospect, of being herafter delivered from the tyranical
and childlike command of the redoubtable little prairie dog.

We now looked forward to a pleasant trip across the American
desart, and though, we were well aware of the frequent privations
we must expect whilst wending our way across its sahara like
extent, we felt that we could brave any danger or difficulty, whilst
led by a person, whose boots were not larger than himself, and
whose pleasure did not consist in mean tyranny, but in social
intercourse with, and frequent approbation of the men under his

command. Throughout the entire route from Bent's fort to Saint Louis,—along the devious windings of the Picquetwah,[3] across the Sierra Ratone,—over the burning plains of the American Desert and along the tortuous deviations of the whole length of the Southern Fork of the Canadian,—Lieut Abert or rather in his capacity at the time, Capt Abert showed himself to be a gentleman in every sense of the term. He threw aside the uncondescion which marked the overbearing exterior of Capt Frémont.—he did not appear like the former to entertain a higer opinion of himself than anybody else did, but on the contrary he rode along with, conversed with,—hunted with his men, and even considered it no disrespect toward himself, for anyone to put on a cleaner shirt.

We enjoyed a slight rain shower whilst here encamped,—but, as soon as the weather cleared up, we geared the mules and saddled our riding animals preparatory for a start.

The 11th,–12th & 13th beheld us encamped within a few miles of the fort, though we altered our position each day, in order to afford good pasturage to our animals, none of which were in any degree rolling with fat or flesh.

On the 14th and 15th we encamped in a little bottom, covered with high coarse grass, near the bank of the river.—The Waltons of our mess employed their leisure time in hooking up catfish from the river, whilst those having an inclination for sporting, sallied out with their rifles, and roamed through the tangled bottoms in search of game.

The river is very shallow in this portion of its course as I have waded it frequently and its greatest depth is about 3 feet.

As the enumeration of our stock of provisions etc, might amuse the reader, we will not consider it out of place, to render the same here.

[3] The Purgatoire River, which flows into the Arkansas near Las Animas, Colorado. Known to the Spanish as Río de las Animas Perdidas (River of Lost Souls), the river became the Purgatoire in French and Purgatory in English, corrupted to Picket-wire in American cowboy lingo. Montaignes' "Picquetwah" is somewhere in between.

In the first place, we had 3 waggons and one carriage,—a 4 wheeled concern, so called by way of distinction. These were laden with Spanish flour,—Rice—Coffee—Sugar,—Tea—and several boxes of Macaroni. The blankets clothing etc of the 35 men made up their cargo. To draw these waggons, there were 4 lean mules secured to each, and a driver to conduct them. There were then 31 mules for the men to ride upon, & in addition to this immense number were about 14 or 15 others, lame, blind and bad & sorebacked, driven along as assistant mules,—in order to have a change of animals in case those secured to any of the waggons, should give out, or fall down in a fit. As for meat to eat, we had a splendid drove of 2 old worn-out hides sent us by our former Captain from the other side of the river.[4]

On the 16th, our little troupe made a longer day's journey than they had yet performed, and arrived about 1 o'clock at the mouth of the Picquetwah. (It flows into the Arkansas about 13 miles below Bent's Fort.) This creek is a muddy little torrent and takes its rise in the Ratone Mountains, its course is from the South West, and the characteri[sti]c features of its banks, are rock bottoms, covered with willow and cottonwood, and high rocky crags covered with dwarf grape vine,—cedar, hackberry and prickley pear. This night, as we encamped on the creek our party was rather unexpectedly increased by the addition of 2 Arapaho loafers who slipped into our camp, unseen by the guards. They remained all night with us yet we missed nothing the next morning.

This being the 17th, we started from the mouth of the Picket-

4 Frémont says the South Company was given coffee and sugar enough for two months, several boxes of macaroni, and a good supply of rice and Mexican flour, as well as eight steers and four circular tents. Abert explains that there had been so many accidents to scientific instruments that he received only a sextant and chronometer and no barometer. He reports the animals at fifty-six mules and seven horses. H. Bailey Carroll calls Abert's party "the great *mulada* expedition across the plains. Perhaps his successes were partly instrumental in making the mule traditional to the U.S. Army." Abert, *Guádal P'a*, 6, 19; Abert, *Journal*, 7; Frémont, *Memoirs*, 426.

wah about 8 o'clock, and after passing a Cheyenne encampment consisting of about 20 lodges,—and meeting a troop of squaws, and papooses mounted on mules and dogs trailing tent-poles behind them, we again encamped on this stream, having come about 13 miles. We were now about 12 from the Fort, and the following day at noon, we were joined by 2 of our men, who had been sent to the fort for beeves, and 3 others, Hatcher.[5]—Greenwood.[6] and Stappe, whereof the 2 former were employed as hunters, to accompany us from Bent's Fort, to that point of the river, whereat formerly stood the trading house, built for the purpose of trading with the Comanches & Kiowas.[7] This we supposed we would reach in 50 days—The other person was one of the other company & had come to take a parting meal with his friends before each struck out in opposite directions. The one towards the East,—the other towards the West.

[5] John L. Hatcher, called by Lewis H. Garrard "the beau ideal of a Rocky Mountain man" in *Wah-to-yah and the Taos Trail,* "had an inexhaustible fund of anecdote and humor." While Hatcher owes much of his fame to Garrard, Abert was also favorably impressed and devotes perhaps more space to Hatcher in his report than he does to Fitzpatrick. Hatcher was born in Botetourt County, Virginia, in 1812 or 1813, and spent much of his early life with a sister in Wapakoneta, Ohio. About 1835 he went to Bent's Old Fort and became a trusted employee of the Bent brothers. At some indefinite time he lived with the Kiowas. After the Abert expedition and the experiences told by Garrard, Hatcher was guide to William Gilpin's command in the closing phase of the Mexican War. He refused to guide Frémont on his disastrous 1848 expedition, warning of its dangers. In 1853 he drove sheep to California with Kit Carson and Lucien Maxwell. In 1859, Hatcher bought a ranch in the Sonoma Valley, California, and about 1867 he moved to Oregon, where he lived in comparative obscurity until his death on his Linn County farm in 1897 or 1898. Harvey L. Carter, "John L. Hatcher," in LeRoy R. Hafen (ed.), *The Mountain Men and the Fur Trade of the Far West,* IV, 125–36.

[6] "Two top hands, one named Greenwood," says Lavender, *Bent's Fort,* 246, is almost certainly not Caleb Greenwood, known as "Old Greenwood," as some have guessed, for Caleb Greenwood was employed from early spring to late fall, 1845, guiding emigrants from Fort Hall to California in the interests of Captain Sutter. Charles Kelly, *Old Greenwood,* 87, 127. Caleb Greenwood had three sons, one of whom, John, incurred his father's wrath over the killing of an Indian. When the father threatened to kill him, John fled from Fort Hall. John Greenwood, twenty-two years old, was known as an excellent hunter and was reputed to be one of the finest shots in the country. While no further evidence supports it, he could possibly have been the hunter of the Abert expedition.

[7] One of the Bents' trading posts, on the Canadian River.

These men brought with them 13 head of Spanish cattle, rations to supply us 13 weeks. We left this place the same evening, not however, before we were serenaded by a large party of Apaches, en route, for the fort. They had taken a scalp, and whilst 3 or 4 strapping drummers sat on horseback & beat their tambourines of stretched buffaloe hide for our edification, an old squaw moved to & fro, over their heads a long pole, at the extremity of which dangled the aforesaid scalp, distended on a kind of hoop or bough. We left the creek on our left and following the Rocky hills, struck off, for the Spanish Trace which leads to Santa Fe from Bent's Fort. We did not attain it this evening; we encamped on a little rocky cleft in the hills, whereat was scant fuel and scantier water, though the ground was covered o'er with a goodly head of prickley pears.[8] We had come 6 miles.

[8] Abert says, ". . . camped at the head of a dry fork, where we found a small pool of water under a rock, but it was so highly impregnated with common salt and sulphate of soda as to be nauseous and bitter to the taste." *Guádal P'a*, 24.

CHAPTER NINE

Wherein The Hole in the Rock and the Hole in the Prairie are talked of—and likewise The Ratone mountaines are described. Herein likewise a stupendous Peak is ascended, and dubbed in the name of all Fools, "Fools Peak." by the ascenders thereof.

The 19th day of August.—The Spanish Trail again.—a Rivulet.—The 20th,—snow seen on the distant mountains,—ceder,—Indian dogs—barren hills,—a prairie thistle,—Soap weed.—used by the people of Mexico.—Black tailed deer,—a Rocky encampment.—The 21st—Hole in the Rock,—Elk,—Hole in the prairie—Shower,—The Ratone and Guadonas [?] in the distance,—the 22nd—The crossing of the Picketwah—Lieut. Peck and wild plums.—his mule—Encamp in a little bottom,—green plums.—Bonnie Black Bess.—Hunters kill a deer—Green wild-plums—dwarf locust.—The 23rd—a gorge of the mountains.—Cedar—pine—fir—oak & cottonwood. —Crosse the Creek Ratone 21 times,—Camp at the foot of a high Peak—a grizzley bear—5 of our party ascend the peak—buffaloe bones and elk-horns,—5 lakes upon a mountain,—Fools Peak.

We left this uncomfortable camping place at an early hour and travelled over an immense plain, which imperceptibly ascended as we progressed towards the South. Numerous prairie dog villages interspersed its monotonous extent, whilst now and then a long-eared hare, started up at our approach & sped away—fleeter than a grey hound. Several sly looking little foxes also stopped in their flight to have a peep at us and towards the middle of the day, a large black wild horse with expanded nostril & streaming mane, came thundering towards [us] across the hot and glaring plain. But when he had approached near enough to discover that we were not of his species, he again made the table ring with the music of his hoofs as he fled across like a gust of wind. Numerous flocks of snow white antelope were also seen in the distance and as our 2 hunters—Hatcher & Greenwood, wended their way over the distant buttes in a course parrallel to our own, several gangs of that peculiar species of deer known as the blacktail[1] ran, frightened, towards us.

The aspect of the country through which we journied this day, was barren and desart in the extreme; and the level plain extending on every side untill bounded by the horizon—the scarcity of water in any receptacle whatever even in the buffaloe wallows,—The hot and parching sun burning the scanty growths of prickly pear and mexican soap-weed into wrinkled specimens of vegetation,—and the wild mustang & unsuspecting antelope fleeing over the wastes,—realized all my conceptions concerning that dismal region which I had formed from the reading of Pike, Gregg, Kemble[2] and geographers who have discoursed thereon.

The distant mountains were now plainly beheld looming in the distance, their peaks extending to the heavens, and mixing with the clouds, and we now felt ourselves on the point of being rewarded for our dreary journey, by obtaining a view of that, El Dorado region of adventurers,—The Mountains. After travelling about 20 miles we struck the Spanish Trail or Road, which leads from Bent's Fort to Taos and Santa Fé, pursuing this for 5 miles we encamped on a small rivulet. The 20th came and passed and though the mountains loomed before us, as though but a few miles distant, we travelled a long day's journey toward [them] &

[1] Note *The Black tailed deer is so called from the peculiarity of the extremity of its tail being of this colour.—Montaignes' note.

[2] Zebulon Montgomery Pike, *An Account of Expeditions to the Sources of the Mississippi, and Through the Western Parts of Louisiana . . .* , 1810; Josiah Gregg, *Commerce of the Prairies*, 1844; George Wilkins Kendall, *Narrative of the Texan Santa Fe Expedition*, 1844.

still they appeared the same distance. The rays of the sun glaring
upon their snow covered summits, gave them the appearance of
huge cones of silver. Leaving the rivulet, we proceeded through a
group of huge, crumbling, hills; their tops covered with clumps of
stumpy cedar, & their sides with great growth of prickly pear &
soap weed.[3] A white Indian dog, looking like a wolf and even
shyer than one, added a feature to the scene which no ways im-
proved its beauty; and though several gangs of black-tailed deer
ran among the hills, the greater part of our route was through a
dreary—silent, inanimate land of sand and soap weeds. Our camp
this night (the 20th) was on the side of a rocky hill covered with
cedar. Here were noticed numerous little formations having the
appearance of iron particles; they existed on the side of this hill
in great quantities, and gave a subject for most animated discussion, to our Lyells and Humboldts. The following morning,
the 21st, we travelled 3 hours to Hole in the Rock;[4] a place so
called from the circumstance of the bed of the small creek or
torrent, being composed of a rough stratum of rock, in the curves
& gaps of which the water is retained in small sheets or little
ponds.—As we started from the morning's camping place,—3
glorious elks,—their enormous antlers resting upon their backs,
—leaped across the rough crags at our approach, and sped away
among the thick cedars.

We watered our animals at the Hole in the Rock & still pursuing
the Santa Fé Trace, reached another famous camping place,
known as the Hole in the Prairie.[5] Here, there was nought but a

[3] The roots of the soapweed or soap plant (*Yucca augustifolia*) were used by
Pueblo Indians and Spaniards as a soap substitute. Abert, *Guádal P'a*, 37.

[4] "Most travelers from Bent's Fort to Santa Fe followed a trail which crossed the
Arkansas some six miles west of the Fort. This trail at first passed through a rough,
broken country of barren hills, and soon reached the headwaters of the Salty Timpas.
The first camp was made at Hole-in-the-Rock, a rocky pool in the bed of this stream,
ringed by dark cedars and huge masses of stone on the slopes about." Vestal, *The Old
Santa Fe Trail*, 255.

[5] Hole in the Prairie was a low, marshy spot, about five miles east of the present
Earl, Colorado. *Ibid.*; Abert, *Guádal P'a*, 28, 69.

few mudholes filled with bad water, yet as, there was no other between this place & the Crossings of the Picquetwah, we were bound to make the best of it & camp. No wood but a few dried weeds—wild sage,—and some scattered Buffaloe-Chips, and a pretty shower of rain about 2 o'clock. The populace of a neighbouring village of prairie-dogs were extremely noisy. The Ratone & Guadon's[6] Mts yet looming in the distance. A band of 13 or 15 elk was seen scudding over the plain, whilst the intervening country between us and the mountains seemed spotted with groups of antelope.

The 22nd We leave "Hole in the Prairie" at the usual hour, and pursue the trail, to the crossings of the Picquetwah. At this place, the stream is about 2 feet deep, very clear and cold, and rushes towards the North West with much swiftness. For some distance its banks were marked by a thick growth of tall cottonwood trees, deadened by the water itself. Many wild plums and black-haw trees overhung the stream & an odd incident connected with the gathering of some of the former fruit happened at this place. Lieutenant Peck, an assistant companion of our Captain, having heretofore rode a tame, patient old mule, who paced along all day, and stopped not except at the will of his master, had, today for a change mounted another quadraped whose disposition was sadly different: it being his usual custom, when left alone by his rider to travel off in such direction as might suit his fancy. When within a mile of the crossings aforesaid, Lieutenant Peck, travelling along the windings of the creek at a distance from the main company, by chance, encountered a most tempting tree, covered with red & luscious plums. As soon as thought, Peck was off, and at 'em. The mule was off too at the same instant, and whilst his master possessed himself of a goodly bough of the fruit, muly was flying like the wind, over the prairie. We beheld the circumstance to advantage and had not several of our generous boys, volun-

6 This name, used twice, probably refers to Wah-to-Yah or the Spanish Peaks.

teered their services, & gallopped away in the pursuit, Peck's mule, saddle, bridle & written observations suspended at the saddle bow, would have been the price of the plums. Fortunately however, the mule was brought in, as we attained the crossings, & Peck, with his plums, was again restored to his recreant steed.[7]

We followed the windings of the Picquetwah, for ten miles; after crossing it, and encamped for the last time upon its banks, in a little bottom filled with growth of wild plum,—and 3 pieces of locust, smaller than that which we see in our own country. Hatcher killed a deer this evening and our fires of dry poles and drift wood, soon warmed our repast of venison & coffee.

The Black mare, whom, in honour to that famous steed of Dick Turpin, I called Bonnie Black Bess, but who rather merited the title of Boney instead of Bonnie, and whom I had thus far led, afforded good proof, of the saying, that a "wild horse is hard to catch" and in return for the trouble I experienced on her account this evening, I saddled her the following day & resolved to use her for the saddle untill, she should become somewhat tamed.

This day's travel was 25 miles.

23rd. Started from the little bottom at half past 6, and entered the gorge of the mountains—on every side, the sides of the mountains were grisly with, fir, pines & scrub oak. The small creek which takes its name of Ratone from these mountains from whose springs it is composed, wound across our route today 21 times. We finally encamped upon its limped waters, at 12 o'clock and resolved to take a rest, preparatory to journeying over the steep hills which lay before us.

A Grisly Bear, was seen today, among the valleys, by our Hunters; but as their quantum of caps & ammunition did not justify an attack upon his fearful personage, they suffered him to go unmolested. A stupendous peak—one which we had noticed

---

[7] The story of Lieutenant Peck and the plums is told also in Abert's journal.

for 4 days,—and one whose foot commenced at our camp of this Evening,—was ascended by a party of 5 of our Company, who desired to render their names immortal. About 2 o'clock, they set out on their perilous enterprise and about ½ past 4 arrived at the summit, without any greater accident than being almost frightened to death, by the sudden appearance of a black tailed deer also frightened by them. They returned at Evening Twilight, bringing with them, in addition to a tremendous elk horn the following information.

"That they had succeeded in gaining the summit by following the gradual ascent of the hills, [until?] at the base of a perpendicular wall about 20 feet in heigth on whose top they mounted by the assistance of one another. A level flat or table lay extended here whilst numerous buffaloe bones and elk horns lay around. They had seen towards the East in the same chain, another high mountain, on whose table like summit were 5 or 6 small ponds or lakes,—They raised a monument of stones at the edge of the rock & dubbed the mountain "Fools' Peak."

The probable heigth of this mountain, above our camp was about 2000 feet, and from the description which our adventurers gave of the inaccessible nature of the summit, the buffaloe bones and elk horns in that queer place, afforded speculative matter for our debate loving messes.[8]

Our men were very careless in leaving the camp and caravan, and usually did so, with uncharged guns, & sometimes without any arms.

Our Explorers of Fools' Peak carried but a single rifle with them to the summit, and the circumstance occasioned some mur-

---

[8] Abert writes: "During the afternoon some of our people made an excursion to a peak which, owing to the peculiar clearness of the atmosphere of the country, appeared very near, but the excursion proved much longer and more toilsome than they had anticipated." Abert sketched the scene with the legend, "Scene near Camp No. 10, Aug. 23rd." H. Bailey Carroll identifies the peak as Fisher's Peak near Raton Pass and south of Trinidad, which is 9,586 feet high. *Guádal P'a*, 32–33 and note 92.

muring at their incautious conduct; "For" observed an old and experienced veteran of the plains, "without a gun, you are not secure even in sight of camp. Many a white men whilst wandering several rods from his friends has been pounced upon by the lurking savages, and even in these very mountains a circumstance happened which well illustrates this fact.

Not many years ago, there were 2 hunters passing through this wild range, and by chance, happened to camp one night at the foot of one of the steep rocks which you will see, tomorrow.

They were experienced men, and knew well that the Indians of the country were no ways backward in attacking a white man for his scalp, and they built but a small fire sufficient to cook their scanty supper. During the night, whilst one slept the other watched his companion & their horses. Before day however, the one who had been sleeping was suddenly awaked by the whizzing of several arrows in dangerous proximity to his body, & with the nimbleness of a squirrel darted forward towards the horses, which had been secured to a couple of small saplings several yards distant.

They were gone,—and pausing but for a moment to behold the body of his comrade as it lay stretched upon the ground, covered with arrows, he made his way down a gloomy but to him secure hollow,—his enemies at his heels with dreadful yells, like a pack of ravenous wolves in pursuit of a wounded deer. He ran for many miles untill, the next day,—He had his rifle & ammunition still with him, exemplyfying all the self-possession of a mountaineer in this respect, and as often as a savage on horseback, showed his person upon a neighbouring butte, he kept his foe at bay, by the presentation of his deadly rifle. 5 times during his route did he discharge that rifle & as often did a warrior tumble from his steed to the ground. During night he crept into some dark hollow or gorge, & after examining his position with a keen eye, he would start on his journey of life, at an early hour the following morning. In 4 or 5 days he reached a Spanish settlement, his barbarous pursuers still in chase of him. "This" continued our Sindbad "was but one of the thousand instances of the sort and I could relate several more, which happened on these very mountains Ratone. I recollect an instance related to me by a friend, which must have taken place near this very Santa Fé Road. 8 trappers and 1 Spaniard as cook for the balance, were moving through these mountains. As they remained encamped at a certain spot, a party of Indians waited upon them & informed them their village was a few miles distant in the valley, & that they were desirous that the white men would pay them a visit at that place & trade with them. The latter were well aware of their duplicity & cunning, & promising to do, as the savages asked, they struck their camp as soon as the red ones had departed & made a move towards a distant peak, on whose summit they expected to be forced to come to a stand.

They had no sooner arrived at the aforesaid peak, and entrenched themselves and their pack animals within a sort of natural fort or barrier, formed of several large rocks, lying in the form of a circle, than the foe came upon them; They were many times more numerous than the little body of trappers, and poured in their arrows upon the latter in thick and fearful hail.

The whitemen were no fools,—and their balls brought down many a naked Indian as he peeped from behind the rocks, and the Spanish cook, having nothing else to do, employed his time in picking up every arrow which fell within the barriers, & breaking it in pieces. "So as the cursed diabolos couldn't shot 'em again." In the hottest of the fight; a tall savage, having doubtlessly become short of arrows, & wishing every remaining one to count, crawled up close to one of the large rocks which defended the brave trappers, and whenever opportunity afforded, rose from his place of concealment, and despatched an arrow at his white enemies. He succeeded in performing this manoeuvre several times, & with great success for an Indian, as he generally contrived to stick an arrow into some one of his pale friends at every pop. Finally as chance would have it—a sharp eyed trapper detected the imposition and placed his rifle along the surface of the rock. The Indian again arose to discharge an arrow; as his swarthy body came before the muzzle of the gun, the white man pulled the trigger, & the Indian chief (for it was he), fell headlong from the rocks.—The balance fled in terror and the courageous trappers pursued their course unmolested.["]

On the 24th, we left this beautiful & picturesque camping place at a late hour, as if loath to abandon its rich scenery, and after scrambling over & down several huge hills or little mountains, we threaded a deep valley, along whose windings curled another beautiful & limped stream, bearing the same name of Ratone as the 1st little stream, yet flowing in a contrary course, and long before the sun had set among the green mountains, we had issued into the great prairie whose borders were from the mountains to the United States Settlements of Missouri & Arkansas. Afar off could we behold the trace towards Santa Fé, meandering over the level plain, not unlike some unterminable tapeline. As we journied along the edges of the mountains before reaching the prairie, our wise men had again subject matter afforded them for long debate, by the appearance of a broken waggon lying at the base of the precipice, and the black & gloomy looks of the pine woods, through whose extent some ravaging fire had raged with exterminating fury. The little valleys were filled with gardens of red cherries, whilst the pure little Ratone ran gurgling from the rough mountains to hide its freezing waters beneath the warm sun of the Rio Rojo; whose waters we encamped about 12 o'clock. It was at this point, but an insignificant creek not more than ten feet in width, and we reasoned among ourselves how many miles would yet have to be journied over by us, before that little creek, would become a rolling river with a channel a mile wide.

We pitched our camp in a clean little bottom, on the river bank, not more than a mile from the place where the Santa Fé Road crosses the Rojo or South Fork of the Canadian.[9]

The cooks of the respective messes were industriously slicing their beef, & making up their bread, whilst the balance set around engaged in idle converse when the cry of "L'ours! L'ours," from the french day guard aroused the camp. I cast my eyes instinctively towards a growth of tall cane-grass, which reared itself among the neighboring cottonwoods, and I beheld the humane physiognomy of a great bear intently engaged in observing the mule which fed unsuspectly within a few rods of his majesty. The shout of the guard, & the rushing forth of so many men, appeared to break the even thread of his charitable reflections, for with us, all at his heels, he made tracks through the river bottom with extraordinary celerity. He escaped with impunity, and was not seen again, except by 2 adventurous bodies Dewey & Linn, who came to the resolve of having a hunt, and for this purpose, took their rifles and sallied down the river. They travelled along for a couple of miles, without being fortunate enough to see any game, & were on the point of returning to the camp, when the idea of setting down to enjoy a rest, occuring to their industrious minds, they forthwith deposited their limbs upon a little green knoll near the river. Their rest was most horribly disturbed it appeared: For a furious and unearthly growl from a clump of bushes near by, brought one to his feet and the other to his legs. Lynn denied most sturdily his having run off; but Dewey being a veracious man, and one who says that Lynn did actually run away from the noise with such exceeding speed as to leave his gun behind, we cannot

[9] Note. The South Fork of the [Canadian] is frequently called Red River or Rio Rojo, from the circumstance of its waters partaly of the colour of the substance of the Soil of the Region through which it passes, which makes it red, as well as from the circumstance of its once having been thought by the spaniards of Northern Mexico, to be the main tributary of or the real Red River itself. The author.—Montaignes' note.

but believe it to be true. Dewey wishing to give Bruin a pill for his toothache, brought his gun to bear upon the bear, and pulled trigger; a most heathenish & diabolical growl was the effect, & the patient thus kindly administered to, rearing upon his hind feet, with expanded jaws and advancing kindly towards Dewey, the Doctor ran away; and so with Linn returned to camp. This was the 2nd and last bear seen by us on our trip.

CHAPTER TEN

Which narrates divers circumstances which took place from the 24th to the last of the month of August. And also how a certain descent of ice bullets came near demolishing the famous little Picquetwah—Ratone—Big Bear—anti-Frémont—Cutnose & Camanche Expedition company.

THE 25th.—A Traveller from Taos—a cache—a mule & Swap,—wild turkies—wolf Shot,—The 26th,—deer & antelope.—Hatcher kills 2—The 27th.—a Santa Fé Caravan of waggons.—The[y] suppose us to be Indians —The Caws,—Camp. a hunt,—rabbits—prickly pears—plums & eagles,—hawks too.—The 28th.—unmeasurable number of antelope—Hatcher kills 2—ponds—ducks & Snipes.—Tremendous hail Storm,—Stampede of men & mules,—a drove of antelope scudding before the Storm—the Cañons.—the torrents,—Camp, —wood. and cold.—The 29th—10 miles travel,—another hunt, —deep chasms.—wolves during the night. The 30th,—Cowheels —Bread & Coffee for breakfast.—wild mule harnessed—a grey

wolf—many villages of prairie dogs.—a green flat.—The 31st.—
Sunday—The edge of the Cañons,—The descent.

Leaving this spot at 7 o'clock the next morning (the 25th), we
crossed the river and left for good, the Santa Fé Trail which we
had thus far followed. However before our starting, an uncouth
looking wayfarer mounted on a mule, rode into our camp.[1] He
was on his way from Taos to Bent's Fort and expected to camp
at Hole in the Prairie, this evening. He swapped the mule he was
riding for another in our Cavejarde—and after giving some of
our boys a treat from a whiskey cache[2] near by, he pursued his
route.

The stream increased gradually in size as we travelled down its
banks, and when we pitched our camp about 2 o'clock in a little
bottom near it, our drawers of water experienced much trouble in
descending its deep black earth banks, and several cases of invol-
untary Baptization occurred as episodes in our monotonous life.
As the little bottom was well filled with copses of thick willows,
and briars, the several turkies which we observed, as we approached, escaped through the tangled wood, with impunity.
Several of our would-be hunters pursued the turkies without

[1] Abert identifies the wayfarer as Robert Fisher, who "gave us useful information
of the country through which we were to pass." Employed by the Bents and St. Vrain
since 1834 or earlier, he was on his way from Taos to Bent's Fort. Born in Virginia
in 1807, he lived in Taos, where he married Maria Rumolda Lopez in 1842. He was
active in the suppression of the Taos rebellion in 1846, and in 1849 he was with
Kit Carson, Dick Wootton, and Antoine Leroux in the unsuccessful attempt to
rescue Mrs. James M. White from Apache captivity. Fisher went to California in
1850 and died there in 1852. Named for him were Fisher's Hole on the Middle Fork of
St. Charles River, later called Mace's Hole and Beulah, and Fisher's Peak, between
Raton and Trinchera passes, presumably the peak of Chapter Nine. Another Fisher's
Peak near Trinidad was named for an army officer. Harvey L. Carter, "Robert Fisher,"
in Hafen, *The Mountain Men*, IV, 97–102; Abert, *Guádal P'a*, 36; Edwin Legrand
Sabin, *Kit Carson Days*, 618–22.

[2] A Cache is a pit made in the ground and lined with hides or grass, for the
purpose of concealing something from the keen eyes of passing Indians. The traders
are often compelled to cache their goods and the trappers their peltries, and in
doing so, find it necessary to make use of considerable cunning & cautiousness.—
Montaignes' note.

success, and during the said Turkey-Chase a large grey-wolf was brought down by Yunt.

Cutting a few willows & brush to place in the bed of the creek and digging down the abrupt bank of either side with our picks—axes—& shovels, we crossed at this point to the other side,[3] on the morning of the 26th. On the side to which we crossed the prairie spread out quite level, & afforded good travelling for our waggons, save when we were compelled by the deep & impassible chasms or gaps which broke the even borders of the river, and forced us to travel around their head or source frequently 6 or even 8 miles distant from the river.—The plain had a more diversified appearance at this portion of the river, than any place which we saw herafter. The numerous chasms branching out from the river,—the numerous forks & tributary chasms of these—and the frequent little green groves which adorned their wild but picturesque scenery,—the hundreds of snow white antelopes, which spotted the green plains & flats, and the frequent dash of some noble deer across the prairie when frightened from his lair by our scouting chasseurs—all made up a landscape, which composed of but few features, on account of its very simplicity exerted a pleasing effect upon us all. Several enormous buzzards could be discerned among the branches of some distant decayed trees on the river banks—spreading forth their sails to dry in the rays of the sun, and though this addition to the beauty of the lancape, cannot, I confess be admired, I shall not deny, but that the lazy—overfed—and dark appearance of these carion birds, assisted much to render this entire Mexican Lancape, peculiarly appropriate to the hot, barren & dismal desart which surrounded it. Our own fair nation, so prosperous & so glorious is represented well by it[s] majestic emblem the proud eaglet,—and as I cast my eyes upon the overfed,—the inert, and yet ravenous buzzard which slowly flapped

[3] The crossing was about three miles south of present-day Maxwell, New Mexico. Abert, *Guádal P'a*, 38, note 108.

its huge wings and the dead branches of the cottonwood, "How appropriate to the Region" I thought "is this Mexican Emblem."

Several gangs of mustangs or wild horses, gallopped around us, and gazed at our caravan curiously from a distance, but not being desirous of improving the acquaintance soon disappeared.

Hatcher killed a doe & fawn towards noon, & furnished our Epicures with a choice bit of venison.[4]

The following day (the 27th) was enlivened by a more important incident, than the death of a deer or the sight of a sleepy buzzard sitting upon a dead tree. We had travelled not more than 5 or 6 miles from our camp of last night, when we observed upon the distant plain, a number of white objects which from the distance, appeared no larger than elk or perhaps deer. They appeared to move, and when we noticed them drive or form into a circle we immediately knew that they were a caravan of Santa Fé waggons En Route for Mexico. We had but just crossed the road, and as my readers may here be rather at a loss to account for the fact of these waggons not pursuing that Trail, which I have heretofore mentioned as, the Santa Fé Trail, and at the same time, our route thus far, I shall inform them at this page, that the route by which we came from Bent's Fort across the Ratone is one trail, and is that which is less frequently followed by waggons from the United States, than the other which is more direct in its course, and which crosses the Arkansas many miles below Bent's Fort. Along this Trail however, there is often a scarcity of water, and at the same time of our sojourn at Bent's Fort, there passed at this point, 16 or 18 waggons. One of our hunters viewed the caravan of waggons from a high sandhill which presented itself upon the plain at no great distance from our route,—and after scanning the party for some moments, established the opinion of their being

[4] Says Abert: "Hatcher shot a fawn in sight of the party. We watched him, half screened in the tall reeds, as he again reloaded, for the doe was so attached to her faun that she seemed reluctant to leave, but was gazing bewildered around, when again the rifle rings, and she too, lay quivering in the agonies of death." *Ibid.*, 39.

Santa Fé waggons. Our 2 hunters, Hatcher and Greenwood, were despatched to the said caravan on a mission of friendship and to enquire the news from the States, whilst we continued our journey over the plain towards the South. Wishing to be joined by Hatcher & Greenwood before dark, we camped on a little ravine about ½ past 2 o'clock & their awaited the arrival of our absent comrades with news. To pass away the hours of evening, a Friend Dewey and myself sallied out with our rifles,—and following the course of the chasm, (I can call it nothing else), we sought for game among its rocks and hollows. Numerous were the caverns & abysses which presented themselves before us,—Immense rocks and walls of rocks lay about in every direction and as I gazed at the overhanging & perpendicular barriers of blackened & mossy rocks above me, around whose summit & sides, flew a brace of screaming eagles frightened by the echoing report of my rifle, I thought of ossa upon ossa[5] and when I again managed to climb to the top, and pick my way over the ragged architecture of nature in her barbarism, I was tempted to look over the edge of the chasm, and gaze at the dark and gloomy scene below. "Tartarus!"[6] thought I. "Fires in its pit and licking its dizzy sides is all that lacks." The smart occasioned by a bed of prickly pears, being disturbed by the pressure of my moccasined feet, assisted the delusion, & I but turned from gazing at Tartarus, to pick a few diabolical spurs from the soles of my erring feet.

The scene was actually wild & dreary in the extreme, and save the screaming eagles which I have mentioned, the silence of these chasms of the Cañons of the Rio Rojo, was unbroken by neither bird nor beast.

"Did ye git som plums?" enquired my anxious comrade at my

---

[5] Ossa and Pelion were mountains in Thessaly which giants in Greek mythology heaped upon Mount Olympus to reach the heavens more easily. "To pile Pelion upon Ossa" is a more common form of the figure.

[6] Tartarus was a region of Hell in Greek mythology. Its entrance was hidden by a cloud of darkness.

elbow, and broke the train of reflections suggested by the scenery below & around me.

I had left him in the hollow, most industriously engaged in masticating and gathering a cap full of the aforesaid plums, and consequently I replied in the negative.

"Thar mout be a few bar in these diggins" mentioned he as he gazed at the chasm, "and" as he looked over the edge, "thar moutn't"

"It looks mighty dismal, down thar" added he "wonder if there arn't the Cañons." "They look awful cruel!" ["]That they do."[7]

Our labours in the chase, as might easily be supposed, were not crowned with any very extraordinary success, and after my friend shooting a hawk & myself blowing a poor, solitary rabbit to atoms, we picked our way, over the rocks & prickly pear back to camp. Here we found some of the boys, engaged in the humane business of prairie dog extermination; (a village of these harmless beings [ ).] It appeared to be a determined matter among us, to attack every individual of the species, who barked at, or shook his tail at us, and it was generally the case, when a village of prairie dogs would be passed, a sufficient corps de chasseurs, would remain in the rear to pepper such of the population as might choose to risk their noisy persons at the entrance of the burrows. On the present occasion the village was very extensive, and small parties of the enemy marched through the streets and discharged their pieces at the several individuals who found oral fault at their unjust proceedings.

Hatcher & Greenwood returned a while before dusk & reported that the caravan was from the settlements, and bound for Santa Fé. That there was no news from the states as they had left Westport at the same time with ourselves. That they had found 2 dead bodies of white men on the route in the region of the Caws or Kanzas & consequently supposed them to have been murdered by

[7] "Bar Peak" inserted here in the manuscript, apparently as afterthought.

that treacherous people.[8] These same Caws or Kanzas, who live in the river known by the same name, are a restless-treacherous tribe. Their propensities for scalping and horse-stealing and in fact all kinds of stealing is purely Indian & natural, but when they persist in carrying on their warfare against solitary Americans, two or 3 & even one individual at a time of that nation from whom, they receive annually money & presents, it marks them as extraordinary knaves and not real Indians. Their is honour even among thieves; and there exists a rude species of honour or ideas of honour, amongst most Indians. They wage continual warfare with all the nations around them, and a Caw Scalp is held in much higher estimation by their friends the Pawnees, than the Kanza himself.

They have committed their depredations on all & the Oregon expeditions have suffered several times from their propensity for horse-stealing. They have taken horses away under the noses of the soldiers at Fort Leavenworth, and we read, but lately, of a party of this villainous & vagabond tribe making off with a number of mules and horses belonging to Chaves[9] the Mexican, whilst at their feeding grounds, near the settlements. The news therefore, brought by the Santa Fé traders respecting the murder of the 2 white men, caused no surprise or doubt, when the place in which they had been found, was said to be the region of the Caws. Our usual day's travel was about 20 miles but for the most part, the length of the day's journey was in proportion to the number of chasms travelled round, or the number of ravines crossed. We

[8] Abert says the hunters reported forty-two wagons, mostly of 5,000 pounds capacity. Names of the owners were Dr. Conelly, Dr. East, Mr. McGuffin, and an "English gentleman of unknown name." Dr. Henry Connelly was active in the Santa Fe trade from 1839 until the close of the Mexican War. H. Bailey Carroll believes "McGuffin" to be James Wiley Magoffin. Abert, *Guádal P'a*, 39–40; Gregg, *Commerce of the Prairies*, 334–35; Louise Barry, "Kansas Before 1854: A Revised Annals," Parts Thirteen–Fifteen, *Kansas Historical Quarterly*, Vol. XXX, Nos. 1–3 (Spring, Summer, and Autumn, 1964), 85, 220, 389.

[9] J. Francisco Chaves, possibly of this family, traveled east on the Santa Fe Trail to attend school in New York in 1847. *Ibid.*, 515.

seldom started before 6 in the morning and generally camped about 2 o'clock; stopping at intermediate hours, only when a welcome pond or hole of water presented itself before us and our thirsty animals; and then only for a short time, to enable all to drink a sufficient quantity of the refreshing element, to last them untill camping hour. We travelled 7 hours on the 28th,[10] and but for an awful hailstorm which commenced about one o'clock & lasted till 2, we would have travelled on untill 3 o'clock. The morning had been most beautiful, and though the bright sun was as fierce as yesterday & seemed ready to consume the scanty herbage of the plain, the sight of several little ponds of rain-water, served to encourage us, and the flocks of snipes and ducks which wheeled around these mirrors of the prairie, brought associations to our mind, at which memory was willing to drop a tear. Antelopes also were still to be seen in great numbers. Hatcher killed a brace. Whilst travelling along at our usual pace, intending to round the source of a certain huge chasm which headed before us, the sky became suddenly overclouded, and the clouds hastened to and fro as if to a dance. It turned out to be a dance sure enough. For after several heavy drops of rain, came down, as if to warn us to prepare for worse, a heavy, freezing, flogging & terrific hailstorm set in and pelted us unmercifully for a whole hour. Many of us were in our shirt sleeves, and our animals goaded on by the descending hailstones, which continued to increase amazingly in size and violence, bore us off before the storm in the direction of the Rojo, regardless of everything, save how to escape the dreadful lashing of the hail.

As is mules' custom, no sooner did the loose ones of which there were 20 odd, feel the iceballs pelting their bones, then turning their heads from the storm, they started off, over the prairie in one stampede. The horsemen were borne along in the rush, and the waggons turning round square from the storm, remained in that

[10] Abert reports twenty-five miles made in these seven hours. *Guádal P'a*, 43.

position untill it was past. The plain was covered with water & iceballs and the loose mules, in their flight, having run off several miles, it was some time, 'ere the whole Cavejarde could be again collected, in marching order.

We camped at the edge of the chasm, instead of passing it, and as we stood almost barefooted (having on a pair of soaked moccasins) in 3 inches of cold water & mud, around a blazing fire, we forgot, in the sight of that element, the discomfort which the other had caused.

T'is said, by some, that such storms are frequent on this river, and may be easily accounted for by the fact of the heated vapours which rise from the hot plains & come in contact with cold clouds from the mountains.[11] They are extremely severe, if they are in general, like the one of the 28th, and must occasion great panic in the timid deer & antelope which are exposed to their fury. During this storm we beheld about 50 antelope in one drove, scudding like lightning over the horizon, to escape from the driving hail. The following morning we journied but a short distance, 9 or ten miles and encamped for the balance of the day, to rest our animals and in some manner recover from the pelting of yesterday.

"Another victory like this, and I am undone" was the exclamation of the ancient hero, and "another hailstorm like this & we are undone" was our opinion.

Taking my gun, I sallied forth to spend the evening, and found, in the appearance of this chasm near which we encamped, nothing very different from that which I described in a former page. The same gloominess,—the same rocky rough sides, and the same wild silent undisturbed scenery. During the night, our vigilant guards were most sadly at a loss to account for divers unearthly yells &

11 Abert comments: "Such storms are of frequent occurrence in the region of the mountains, where the clouds are constantly forming, by the warm currents of the plains meeting with the cool moisture condensing atmosphere which hangs around the summits of these snow-capped mountains." *Ibid.*, 28.

noises proceeding from the plain, which, they felt confident, was occasioned by no others than Indians.

We had slaughtered a beef in the evening and when morning came, his entrails etc had been entirely demolished by the wolves. This explained the night's yells and noises, and if there existed any satisfaction in the act, I was gratified the following morning by having a noble shot at one of the lurkers of the night who was still gliding around for more prey.

The 30th beheld us at a luxurious dejeuner of boiled cow heels, —Bread & Coffee,—dainty sup for this region. We started on our journey at 7 o'clock, and instead of renewing it over a level unmarked plain, we ascended & descended over several ranges of hills or buttes running East & West. Numerous villages of marmots still interspersed the Region, and as we attained a swell of the plain,—a little flat of a circular form, and covered with a greener clothing than the surrounding country spread out before us, & afforded beautiful pasturage to many flocks of antelope, & a play ground for many prairie dogs, whose houses were around its edges, and who frisked & gamboled around as if desirous of passing their time in amusement only.

The place also, bore many & evident marks of serving as a race course and a feeding ground to gangs of wild horses.[12] The soft soil was literally covered with their hoof tracks. There were 6 or 8 seen by us within a few miles distance, looking noble enough to be sure, whilst loose upon the plain, but if caught and placed before a heavy waggon, soon a miserable drudge,—complete.

We passed over several beds of creeks or torrents, which were as usual perfectly dry: along their banks were quantities of grapes—plums etc, & among the brush and underwood, some deer & rabbits.

[12] Abert: "*Equus calealus*, which naturalists agree have originated from the stock introduced by the Spaniards. The Indians we meet use them for riding, while others only pursue and take them for the meat ... which is said to be well flavored and preferable to that of the antelope." *Ibid.*, 44–45.

The 31st. Sunday and the last day of August 1845. Started at 7 o'clock and ascend rather gradually towards a point ahead. Follow a sort of dividing ridge high and narrow, between several petite chasms or gaps and reach, about 9 o'clock the edge of the great precipice,—a complete mountain.—T'was the finale of the Cañons.

The Cañons of the South Fork of the Canadian, or the Rio Rojo, are famous with all the traders and explorers who have ever passed through this region, and are well worthy of description. The term Cañon is Spanish & applied to that portion of the river, which is confined on each side by stupendous barriers or walls perpendicular,—and the word Las Cañons is more particularly bestowed on that portion of the Rio Rojo, below the crossings of the Santa Fé Trail, where the water is confined on either side by a great rocky wall, in some places 500 feet perpendicular. All access to the water of the river is of course impossible for animals, and when travelling down the stream as we were, travellers are compelled to keep off, from its banks, some 6 or 8 miles & even ten, in order to pass the great rents which run out on either side from the rocky barriers. These Cañons are between 50 and 60 miles in length, and for 3 or 4 days, we had been passing them. We now arrived at the point, where they term[inate] and though still at a considerable distance from the river, a steep and lengthy precipice was yet to be descended, in order to again reach the even plain.

We fastened our riding animals to the few trees around, and prepared to let down the waggons to the first shelf some 60 yards below, by hand.

Long ropes were secured to the rear of the waggon and after the draught animals were taken out, we let them down one by one, all hands assisting together.[13]

---

[13] Abert notes that the descent, suggested by Fitzpatrick as most practical and safest for men, animals, and equipment, was completed in six hours. *Ibid.*, 46.

In this manner was the first descent made. The mules were again put to them, and the path through the rocks, being prepared by the men, the drivers by careful management contrived to attain the 2nd ledge. We were still at some distance from the bottom and 3 of the frail vehicles had already commenced the last descent which connected with the plain, when the last, coming in contact with a sturdy rock, snapped its tongue. Here indeed was an accident. The balance were ahead,—There were but 3 or 4 pack-saddles in the Company, and the waggon had a considerable load. The tongue was beyond all repair: and the draught mules were speedily adorned with pack saddles. By means of a stout thong, to confine the tongue in its place, the empty waggon was transported to the plain. The mules with packs were driven down after the balance, & all promised well to go on to the next camp without any more accident. The hour was passing on towards evening and all were anxious to reach water, but from the arid appearance of the plain, we despaired of finding water or wood within the limits of the horizon. One of the mules, and one with a pack—a sack of coffee—being unused to such burthen, or being too well used to it, resolved to ease himself of it, and leaving the balance darted among the rocks & hollows, and was soon beyond sight. Coffee is a precious article in this region, & we explorers could not thus part with it, and knowing that the mule would throw it over the rocks or throw himself along with it, a party therefore obtained a more docile animal, and set in pursuit of the mule and coffee. The mule was not found, but as expected, the sack of coffee and packsaddle were, and again placed upon a mule.

By this time, the caravan was far in advance of us, and we could see from our elevated situation among the rocks, the train of our little Company, winding over the prairie, in a direction from us, at the distance of 4 or 5 miles.

About an hour before sunset, a stream of water, with one cottonwood tree in sight, was reached and we pitched our camp. The recreant mule was already there.

CHAPTER ELEVEN

Which embraces the Events of one week on the Desart, and wherein mention is made of Bald-Head.

SEPT. 1st. — Sandhills. — Road-making.—Red water.—few antelope.—Small stream of Coloured water.—Lose powder horn & Shot-bag.—Fitz & Hatcher go out as scouts.—Return at dusk & their report.

Sept. 2nd.—Cross the little stream—travel till 2—a broken country, few small streams.—great growths of prickley pear, —clump grass.—wild horses.—Antelope—Rattlesnakes.—Red River again—grapes,—wild turkies—pit and ancient windlass seen by Yunt.—green fruit on divers trees. Wild turkey killed.

3rd September. Pickets easily pulled out by the mules.—Old Mexican trail.—old axle trees.—prairie plums—Camp at ½ past One o'clock.—A fire on Red River.—hackberries and partridges,—the prairie on fire for 8 or ten miles.—Old La Tulippe's croaking thereupon.—A hunt with Janvier.—a delicious spring and luxuriat bottom.—a farm & several wild turkies.—Sandhills.

Sept. 4th. Patrick's mule—Pater—shows a few gymnastics at starting,—another old axle tree.—Direction East.—Still pursue the old Trail.—reach a little grove and a spring about 20 miles off.—hunt with Russel.—Raven Roost—sandburrs—deer & buffalo-horns and plenty of plums.—Caral of trees,—plum pudding. —Sleeping on Guard.

Sept 5th. Leave plum-pudding Grove & follow the old Trail 6 miles north East.—Become dubious of its destination and strike off from it in a South East direction.—3 Indians seen by Fitzpatrick—antelope,—a deer killed.—prairie dogs.—a spring—Rockey edge of the Rojo.—turn back 4 miles and encamp on the Spring branch.—Bete-puant—deer killed by Hatcher.—Ventriloquism extra.

Sept. 6th—Wild-Turkey-Roost.—Bucephalus in gears.—fresh Indian trail.—cross hollows, thread valleys and mount hills.—3 deer.—Caral—Break down of Yunt's waggon—Course N. East. —Red River.—selon Hatcher, the trail passed today at 12, was that of about 100 lodges.—200 warriors. (Camanches). and most probably the band of old Bald-head, as his, is the only clan having regular lodges,—The balance having temporary shelters of branches & bark.—The signs used by the prairie tribes to make known their meaning.[1]

Sept 7th.—Sunday—ascent of the hills,—an Indian war trail.—signs of buffaloe.—ducks in the River.—we camp in a bottom—mosquitoes in great numbers.—no sleep.—beef killed.—Night—Bathing in the Rojo.

The damaged waggon being repaired, and all hands having been refreshed by a good sleep and hearty breakfast, our little Exploring Company left the little creek, and wended its way over the flower covered prairie towards the South East.

We travelled for 6 hours, and in passing over a ridge of rough sandhills,—and rain ploughed furrows, were frequently compelled to make use of the pick & shovel. Few antelope could now be seen, and when we pitched our camp about 2 o'clock on a little creek of red-water,[2]—there was not a living object to be discerned between us & the circle of the horizon. This evening our pilot and

---

[1] The signs are discussed in Chapter Twelve.

[2] Abert says a grove of large cottonwoods and a natural meadow of tall grass made this one of their best camps. *Guádal P'a*, 49.

campmaster—Fitzpatrick and Hatcher the hunter, rode out among the distant hills for the purpose of discovering whether any human beings were near. We were now, unquestionably in the Camanche & Kiowa Region, and as we had not beheld heretofore a single individual of either tribe, we now expected to behold some in a few days.—They returned at dusk, and reported that they had beheld a smoke towards the East about 12 miles distant, and gave it, as their opinion that we would see Indians on the morrow. The little rivulet upon which we camped, was not more than 3 or 4 feet in depth and in some places not more than that many inches, but as its banks were abrupt and frequently 12 or 14 feet perpendicular, we found it necessary to dig down on either side, the following morning, to make way for our troublesome little waggons. The bottom also was composed of quick sand, and we cut a quantity of willows & cane grass & threw in at the crossing. The country travelled over by us today, was very broken, and intersected with several small creeks of good water, all of which flowed towards the East & South East.—Enormous growths of prickley pear of various species, and clumps of tall grass thinly scattered over the swells was the sole vegetation to be seen, whilst a few wild horses and 3 antelope who ran up very close to us, as if glad to see human beings, formed the living population. Rattlesnakes also abounded, and we were much gratif[ied] to see the river once more before us about 2 o'clock. It was here flowing Eastwardly, and though yet confined between very high banks, its aspect was more cheerful, than we had seen it for some time. We camped in a little bottom, beneath the shade of the cottonwoods, and refreshed ourselves by a bath in the cool waters and the enjoyment of eating some fine grapes, of which there existed quantities along the Rojo. Several wild turkies were seen & some killed.—a pit and an ancient windless on the South side, were noticed by a couple of our men, and supposed to have been the work of Mexicans,—seeking water during an extraordinary drought perhaps. There was also, at this place, a kind of tree which bore a nut or bean of queer appearance, growing in clusters or bunches of 6 or 8, each of which was a nut or bean looking like a round gravel, & covered with a transparent, yellow, glutinous, resinous coating which, being chewed, conveyed a sweet sensation to the palate, & a bitter one on to the lips and tongue. The leaves of the tree were oblong and scolloped at their edge. and the tree itself was never of great size or heigth. It may be well know[n], but, I have never seen the same in any other country of the west.[3]

The bottom was loose & sandy, and when on the following morning (the 3rd) we discovered that half of the mules had drawn their pickets and were roaming at large, it occasioned no surprise. We saddled our animals and striking out from the river, pursued an ancient trail,[4] which had not been travelled apparently for years, & which had been made, no doubt, by Mexican traders crossing the region towards the Kiowa country. We followed it all day, and when it finally approached near the river, we pitched our tents in a sloping little bottom, and spent the balance of the evening in exploring the country around in search of novelties and game. Of the former there were several,—curi-

[3] The Pride of India, *Melia azederach*, commonly known as the Chinaberry. A native of India and Persia introduced into the southern part of the United States early in the nineteenth century and since naturalized throughout the South, its rapid growth and green foliage, which it retains until late in autumn, make it a desirable shade tree. During April the *Melia azederach* produces numerous lilac-colored flowers. These are succeeded by a crop of yellowish, translucent berries. The wood, although coarse, is durable, and the tree can withstand a fairly low temperature. Liberty Hyde Bailey, *Cyclopedia of American Horticulture*, II, 1001. Abert describes the Pride of India as a tree not more than thirty feet high, covered with a yellow fruit containing a single nut with a pulpy exterior "exceedingly disagreeable to the taste, and so pungent that it was a long time before I could get rid of the unpleasant impression it produced." *Guádal P'a*, 50.

[4] Abert calls this point the "Spanish Crossing," where the Comanchero trail crossed Ute Creek at its junction with the Canadian River. He says that "two deeply cut ruts gave to the trail the appearance of a wagon road, but their sometimes variable parallelism showed that they were formed principally by the feet of passing animals." (*Ibid.*, 51, note 157.)

ous rocks,—several caves,—a deserted Indian village[5] and a beautiful spring which burst out about a mile below our camp, from a bed of snow-white sand, and formed the source of a considerable rivulet which wound through the verdant and luxuriant bottom, untill it emptied into the river. Of the latter, there was but a scanty variety; a flock of partridges whistled around our tents and as a couple of us wandered along the bottom in the neighbourhood [of] the beautiful spring above mentioned, a flock of wild turkies crossed our path, and a young faun bounded through the copse. About 4 o'clock, the high grass which surrounded our camp, was fired by the carelessness of a cuisinier-noir, and had not the wind been in an advantage[ous] direction, our tents and waggons would not have escaped with impunity. As it was, the flames dashed down the bottom through the dry & crackling grass, and the heavy fire went roaring & smoking for 8 and ten miles perhaps 20. The scanty clump grass which grew upon the sandhills was licked clean by the devastating element, and as far as we could see the edge of the river, and the prairie was flaming fearfully.[6] "Les sauvages seront vous frentot," remarqued old La Tulippe, the veteran of 50 winters passed in the montaigns and the Fur Trade. "Pour trouver un sauvage, faites un boucane."[7]

On the 4th, we made a start over the sandhills and again pur-

5 Abert calls it an "old Spanish camp" rather than a deserted Indian village, saying: "There we found a few poles, upon which some withered leaves still remained, showing they had been cut this season, and the pickets to which the animals had been attached were still standing." *Ibid.*, 51.

6 Abert notes that from their camp the following evening they could see "immense columns of smoke . . . rolling upward to the sky" and that smoke could be seen for several days thereafter. He attempted to emphasize to his men the dangers of prairie fires, caused by carelessness. *Ibid.*, 53, 56.

7 François La Tulippe, or Tulipe, was a veteran of Frémont's first expedition. In 1842, La Tulipe had been one of a party of trappers who, attempting to boat their furs down the Platte but finding the water too shallow, had cached their furs and were walking toward St. Louis when they met the Frémont party. La Tulippe was easily persuaded to accompany the Pathfinder. His (or Montaignes') fractured French is not translatable, but the general sense is, "The Indians will soon be with us. To find an Indian, build a cooking fire." Frémont, *Memoirs*, 75, 169; Grinnell, *Trails of the Pathfinders*, 398; Goetzmann, *Army Exploration*, 77.

sued the ancient trail, which, our opinion of its being a Mexican trail, was confirmed by the appearance of several weather beaten axle trees along the route. There was one at the spring, I mentioned. As a petite Episode in the usual business of the day, Pater (Patrick's mule), resolved to have some amusement at the expense of his rider, & to carry out his views, carried Patrick through the rude limbs of a grisley hackberry tree.

Our course was nearly East, and was over a country—more rolling than we had lately been passing. In the hollows were grapes and hackberries and upon the swells were plums innumerable. About 2 o'clock a grove of cottonwoods hove in sight, and finding a spring of water beneath them, we unsaddled our animals and pitched our tents.

As plums were abundant in the neighbourhood and as a few grapes were fortunately discovered in time, it entered the minds of certain individuals to have a plum pudding. Before sunset several of us took a stroll around, and came across a tremendous buzzard roost and an extensive garden of that pesty burr, the sandburr. Deer & buffaloe horns were likewise scattered about, and when we returned at sunset, a caral[8] of felled trees was formed for our defence, in case of an attack from the Indians whom we supposed were lurking about.

The plum pudding as usual had bad consequences, and when the sun arose, on the 5th, it was bruited about that one of the plum pudding eaters had been detected asleep during his guard.[9]— Leaving this plum-pudding grove, we again travelled along the

[8] Abert tells how Fitzpatrick taught the men to construct a corral by "felling large trees and arranging them in such a manner as to describe the arc of a circle, interlacing them with small branches . . . the remainder of the circle completed with wagons and tents." If timber was not available, the corral would be built against a bluff, bank, or deep ravine. *Guádal P'a*, 53.

[9] Abert says "one of the messes made . . . a nondescript pudding, which had it not been for the fruit, one might liken to sailor's duff. They kindly sent some to our mess, and, at that time, we thought it excellent." He makes no mention of a man asleep on guard. Possibly Montaignes exaggerated. *Ibid.*

old Mexican trail for 8 miles, untill percieving that it bore North East, and almost in a direction at right angles with the Rio Rojo, we left it on our left & struck off towards the river in a South Eastern course. Several antelope were seen today,—Hatcher killed a deer, and Fitzpatrick related having seen 3 Indians in the distance. We passed a spring about 2 o'clock, and travelled forwards towards the river.—We found it impossible to reach it by reason of the rocky edges & deep chasm, and forthwith retraced our steps to the spring branch we had crossed a couple of miles back. Here a most unsavoury odour was occasioned by the death of a bête-puant, and pardon our taste, kind reader, when I say that a portion of our company enjoyed themselves finely on the soup manufactured from the said bête-puant.[10]

This Evening was passed off most delightfully in conversation, ventrioloquial exhibitions,—songs & a polecat supper.—A wild turkey roost stood near our encampment but the cunning birds did not approach it during our sojourn at the place.

On the morrow (6th) we started at 7 o'clock, & though there was some little delay caused by an Indian pony being placed in gears, we managed to perform a good day's travel. About 12 o'clock we crossed a wide Indian trail, which, selon[11] Hatcher who was good authority, was that of 100 lodges or 200 men, moving their village, and most probably Camanches,—the band of old Bald-Head, as this is the only one having regular lodges. The balance makes use but of temporary shelter formed of brush or bark. We crossed many hollows or valleys and ascended and descended numerous sandhills. 3 noble deer bounded over the yielding ridges at our approach.

The 7th, being Sunday, we made an early start, and the broken

---

[10] Says Abert: "In one of the crevices of the rocks we found a polecat, *Mephitis Americana* . . . . The French people who were with us caught it, and ate it. The odor, however, was too pungent to suit every one's olfactories." *Ibid.*, 54.

[11] The use of *selon*, a French preposition meaning "according to," is another example of Montaignes airing his presumed French background.

waggon being repaired,[12] we travelled over the hills at a good-gate. We crossed an Indian war trail, and beheld numerous signs of recent buffaloe having been about. We beheld likewise gangs of wild ducks upon the river. Stopping only to give our animals water at the bend of the river, we dug a road across several deep gullies, and camped about 2 o'clock in a bottom. We had but little sleep tonight,—mosquitoes were humming & singing in every direction. A beef was killed,—the meat was jerked partly & several bathed at night in the cool water of the Rojo.

CHAPTER TWELVE

Which relates numerous circumstances, as also Red River,—Red-water—Red men & Red Coffee

THE 8th.—Buffaloe Bulls,—500 Buffaloe in a band.—Hatcher kills a cow. Bosse and Bosse Caps.—Camp on the River.—Mosquitoes.—Roasting & boiling.—Hatcher sees 2 Indians.—Catfishing by Yunt & Company.—An Indian village deserted.—wild turkies,—Rain,—guard.—9th Sept. Rains all day.—remain encamped.—Road making.—Black root and Gunpowder.—Yunt & Co fish to day.—Red Coffee—Great rise in the River.—Indians seen by Fitzpatrick.—They approach.—Their report etc.—their mode of eating.—they are Buffaloe Eaters.—Comanches divided into several bands.—Their departure.—wild turkey shot by Greenwood.—Rain & wind. The 10th Sept. Pass around the foot of the bluffs.—deep gullies and

---

[12] In his summary preceding this chapter, Montaignes mentions the "Break down of Yunt's waggon" occurring on September 6. Abert reports that a wagon tongue was broken on September 6. *Ibid.*, 55.

ravines.—Buffaloe Bull Shot by Hatcher.—one Indian seen.—
plums & grapes—The Semirone or Cimarone,—The Beaver.—
The waters of the Rio Rojo are unhealthy.—Indians usually encamp at a distance from it.—The trading house.—The Camanches and Cayquas compared.—The Osages, and Hatcher's story
of the Pawnee on the Platte.—Arrow Creek.—Elk Creek.—Buffaloe Creek.—Cutnose & Big Tree or False Ouachita.—The Big
Spring on the prairie between the Cimarone and Arkansas.—Harden's waggon.—The Camanche Chiefs in Texas.—The Apaches
—The Texian Cowboys.—Hatcher Bravado adventure with the
Governor of Santa Fé.—Our camp in a Bottom,—grapes—plums
—snipes & cool wind.

As we journied along the windings of the river today (the 8th,)
we were frequently forced to use the shovel and pick, in order to
cross deep revines ploughed by the torrents in their descent into
the river. Several buffaloe bulls appeared in the distance, and
about 1 o'clock, as we gained the edge of a high hill, a band of
buffaloe, about 500 in number, appeared near us. Hatcher killed
a cow, and bringing the meat thereof to the camp, he with 2 others,
returned in pursuit of the band. They had admirable luck, and
returned at dusk with 2 mules well packed with choice bits.—
Ribs,—brisket and Bosse.[1] This latter part, is that portion of the
animal called the hump, above the shoulders and is esteemed a
greater delicacy than the tongue. The circula[r] & concave skin
which covers it, forms when dressed a warm, but barbarous looking head piece, and nothing less than a ferocious Bosse cap must
satisfy our Adonises who strutted about camp with an air of

---

[1] "In butchering, the skin is cut open on the back, and the meat on each side of the
long spines of the vertebral column, termed the 'fleece' is then removed, and the
spines themselves, broken off close to the vertebra, form that part called the 'hump
ribs,' a favorite part; then comes the 'bass,' just back of the neck, the side ribs, and
tongue. The remainder is generally left to the wolves. Sometimes the large bones of
the legs are brought in for the marrow, which, when roasted, is delicious; much
resembling butter, and of a deep yellow color." Abert, *Guádal P'a*, 57–59.

109

concious superiority in looks. Our camp was between the bluffs
and the river, and near by a large village or remnants of a village
long since abandoned by its savage inhabitants. The mosquitoes
were not at all scarce in this quarter, and they commenced their
orchestra at an early hour. There were some few catfish in the
river and certain Isaac Waltons of our messes employed their
leisure hours in conveying the same from their cool element
[into] the warmer atmosphere of the frypan. The scene of roasting and boiling and jerking which always follows a successful
buffaloe hunt was in no manner disturbed by the fear of lurking
Indians, though Hatcher reported having seen 2 today, whilst
in pursuit of the bison. Towards dusk several wild-turkies approached camp and one was shot by Greenwood. Rain began to
fall at dark & continued during night.

The following day (the 9th) was also a rainy one, and we
remain encamped at this place. The bluffs approached the edge
of the river and barely left sufficient space between for the passage
of wheeled vehicles. Even this was obstructed with great rocks,
and during the day, we employed ourselves in removing them.
Yunt and Company again pursued their piscatory employment
and towards evening a mess of small cats crowned his labours of
the day. At a late hour of the day, Mr. Fitzpatrick as usual ascended the high cliffs or bluffs which reared their summits above
us, and soon returned with the tidings that Indians were about.
At the same instant a solitary savage mounted on horseback appeared on the summit of a crag about 1½ miles distant,—another
soon joined him, then another untill 6 or 8 were in sight. We
hoisted a signal and waved it to & fro, as a sign of friendship.
They rode to and fro along the hills as if dubious of our inten-
tions. We continued to wave the mosquito bar, and they finally
came to the conclusion to approach us. They did so however, with
great cautiousness & whilst one or 2 of their old men rode into
camp, the balance (There were ten or 12) remained at a distance

untill they saw all was friendly & even then came in one after the other, as if yet but half-convinced.[2] They turned out to be a party of Buffaloe-Eaters,—a tribe of the Camanches—there were 3 or 4 squaws among them,—weather beaten damsels, and they reported their village to be about 6 or 7 miles distant on the Creek which emptied into the river above. According to them, the old trading post to which we were going was but 2 or 3 day's travel distant,—the Kioways were farther down on the river, and the tribe of old Red Shirt the Camanche. They could make use of some few Spanish words, the principal of which was nada & buena —picked up by them from such traders as trafficked among them and during their expeditions towards the South, and together with these and the manual signs[3] which constitute the standard language among all the prairie tribes,[4] they managed to inform us the

[2] As the Comanches approached, Fitzpatrick rode to meet them and persuaded them to accompany him to the camp. *Ibid.*, 60.

[3] Note. The signs used among the Indians to express their ideas to each other are various and very expressive. drawing the fingers across the brow,—holding up the 2 clenched hands,—shaking the 2 hands at the Ear,—holding up two fore fingers—holding down the 2 fore fingers,—holding the stretched hand towards the ground & trailing it along in a meandering direction.—striking the left breast with the ends of the right fingers.—bending the hands inwards & motioning towards the earth with the fingers.—pointing to the sun & to different points of his course.—are several of the signs in use among these tribes and respectively signify—white man— mountains.—mule,—pawnee or wolf.—dog.—Camanche or Snake.—Arapaho.—village or encampment.—day or parts of a day etc etc. F. des M.—Montaignes' note. [See also: William Philo Clark, *The Indian Sign Language*; William Tomkins, *Universal Indian Sign Language*; Iron Eyes Cody, *How: Sign Talk in Pictures*; and Robert Hofsinde, *Indian Sign Language*.]

[4] Note 2nd. The Camanches are divided into several bands or clans. as for example: Buffaloe Eaters.—horse Eaters.—Hoes etc.—Root Eaters. They all eat Buffaloe meat, & those known by the distinctive cognomen of Buffaloe Eaters, follow this animal in his march North & South, & whilst he feeds on the green prairies of Mexico, the villages of these Camanches are not far distant. F. des M.—Montaignes' note. [Comanche bands were autonomous groups, loosely organized, each centering its activities in a vaguely defined territory. They were not antagonistic toward each other, and bands and their members intermingled freely. There were differences in speech, customs, dances, and dress. The Buffalo-eaters, or Kotsotekas, generally roamed in the Canadian valley. Montaignes' Hoes also appears as Ho'is, meaning Timber People, but this band, one of the largest, is more commonly called Honey-Eaters, or Penateka, or Wasps. They were farthest south and most isolated of the Comanche bands, and the only band that supplied scouts to the troops fighting other

above. A present of tobacco was made them, and they were invited to partake of our supper of bread, rice, coffee & buffaloe meat. They fell to, at the sight of the victuals, and each one seizing a different dish, and began a system of masticatory demolition which would have charmed Heliogabalus himself.[5] They had several fine steeds among them, and several mules, all of which were doubtlessly of Mexican birth. They left us to return to their village, and we again returned to our roasting, boiling and jerking, though Yunt & Co. could not recommence their fishing. The rain which had fallen during the greater portion of the day, having occasioned a sudden rise in the Rojo, which caused that river to dash along its channel with exceeding swiftness, foaming like a boiling pot.

It is not out of place, to mention a circumstance which cannot be read without a strange feeling of doubt: to wit, that the Camanches steal & their neighbours the Kioways or Cayquas do not. I mention this on the authority of one who has had numerous opportunities of testing its truth and one who has for years been a trader among both nations.[6]

The morning following the visit of the Buffaloe-Eaters (the

Comanches. The Yamparikas, or Yap-eaters, ate a potato-like root called yap by Comanches and yep by Shoshones. They lived farthest north. Others were the Wanderers, Liver-eaters, Antelopes, Tenawa or Down Stream band, and Burnt Meat band. Montaignes' term Horse Eaters may have been a variant name for one of these bands. Edward Adamson Hoebel, *The Political Organization and Law-Ways of the Comanche Indians*, 1940; Rupert Norvel Richardson, *The Comanche Barrier to South Plains Settlement*, 1933; Ernest Wallace and E. Adamson Hoebel, *The Comanches, Lords of the South Plains*, 1952.]

[5] Heliogabulus was the Roman emperor M. Aurelius Antoninus, so called because he adopted the worship of a Phoenician deity so named. The emperor was known for his licentiousness and extravagances. Abert reports that his Indian guests enjoyed the food, but expressed a decided dislike for the coffee. *Guádal P'a*, 60.

[6] Montaignes' authority is probably John Hatcher. Abert also comments on Kiowa honesty: "The Kioways sustain a character for bravery, energy, and honesty, while the Comanches are directly opposite, being cowardly, indolent, and treacherous. The Kioways are particularly noted for their honesty; and while we remained with them nothing was stolen—an occurrence sufficiently uncommon to merit special notice." *Ibid.*, 66.

10th), we again set in motion, and passing around the foot of the bluff beforementioned, left the river on our right, & wended our way across gullies and hills unnumerable filled with growths of plums & grapes. A buffaloe bull was shot by Hatcher during the day[7] and a solitary Indian was observed on the distant buttes. This evening we encamped on the river, and though the water was very bad, impregnated as it was, so strongly with red clay & sand, in want of better, we were compelled to make use of it for coffee. The water of the Rio Rojo is said by those who have travelled & sojourned upon it & who of course have experience of the same, to be unhealthy, and even the Indians, who are very Stoics in regard to every thing of the kind, are generally loath to pitch their villages on its banks, and for the most part seek a place on some clearer tributary or spring. We expected to reach, in a week's travel at furthest, the old trading post on the river, whereat Hatcher and Greenwood's journey would finish, and as each day passed by, the former remarqued various changes and appearances in the river, which confirmed him in this opinion. The post in question, was but a species of rude log or block house into which, the trader at certain periods of the year, conveyed his goods, and at which all the trading for robes and furs, was carried on untill the Indians' stock of robes were exhausted. Then, after burning the house or fort, in order to prevent other traders from making use of it, he would return to the states with his robes, to exchange for money & more goods. To this fort would the Camanches and Cayquas annually resort to traffick their hunting spoils, for beads, bells, wire, vermillion, cotton handkerchiefs, tobacco & trinkets. Our hunter informed us that once upon a time, a party of Pawnees approached the fort, and signified their intention to trade. But as they are a treacherous people, he bade them keep off,

---

[7] This buffalo had been injured in combat with another bull. Abert writes: "He had left the herd to die alone, for the wound would have proved mortal, and the death he owed to us only put an end to prolonged suffering." *Ibid.*, 62.

or he would fire upon them. "To tell the truth which has long been found out" added he "These pawnees are the greatest rogues of the prairie. I was once descending the Platte in a boat, in company with several others, when, one evening, a party of these Indians appeared at the edge of the shore & told us to land. We did not mind them for some time,—they continuing to follow along the shore. At last one of them a strapping big fellow, as tall as an Osage, ran out on a point of land in advance of us, and I resolved to let him come aboard. We got him in, and rowed on down the stream. The devil however wished us to land him here & there, & whenever we rowed up to one place, to suffer him to get ashore, he said that was not the place and told us another one. We soon became tired of this, and when, after landing 3 or 4 times to suit his whims, I bade him keep still for I was not going to land him at all. He chattered around a good deal at this, & vowed, I expect, deep vengeance against us. Finally I could withstand his entreaties to land him, no longer, and catching him by the neck & leg, threw him into the river.["] The whole set of prairie tribes are a wild & rascally set, and an Arapaho or a Chienne as bad as a Camanche or an Apache, and a Pawnee is worse than either. As for the Apaches, the[y] for the most part hang around the skirts of the Spanish settlements & confine their depredations to that region. The Comanches have received a grievous panic at the slaughter of their 60 chiefs at San Antonio de Bejar, and the Cayquas carry on their warfare in North Mexico, against the Cavejardes and Ranchos. They however are not the only depredators which the pusillanimous Mexicans have to fear. The Cowboys of Texas formerly carried on a profitable warfare against Spanish horses mules, & cattle, and the charitable Camanches, Apaches & Cayquas, as also the Chiennes, still follow up the profession. As an instance of the cowardly and pusillanimous, (an appropriate word), character of the Mexicans of North Mexico, I shall here give ad verbatum, the bravado adventure of a trader in Santa Fé several years since.

"I went out with a venture of goods to Santy Fee about —— years ago, and with 6 or 7 men entered that town. My goods were contraband or such as were subject to a heavy duty, and as I expected, were immediately seized by the orders of the governor. I immediately hastened to his quarters and told him that I was an American, & would have my goods back. He replied they were contraband, & should not enter his territory without heavy duty. I told him I would give no duty, but would have my goods back. I continued to curse and lash myself into a passion, as he thought and to increase the effect of my demonstrations, yelled Arapaho like a veritable barbarian and drew my knife. The governor was standing at the other extremity of the room, & when he heard me shouting in an unknown language, he asked if that man was getting mad. One of my men replied that I was, & that when I did I was a fiend incarnate. ["]Tell him, then," said he, "not to talk that way any more but to take his goods and trade.["]

CHAPTER THIRTEEN

An Incident on the Rio Rojo.
"Environed 'round with nature's shames & ills,
Black heaths, wild rocks, black crags & naked hills."
Wonders of the Peak

2 INDIANS turn in as we turn out of Camp.—The old Beef.—The hills and petrifactions.—gullies —chasms—hills,—walls—barriers and precipices.—grapes &

115

hackberries.—a war party of Kiowas.—A Spaniard among them.
—Travel till 4 o'clock.—one tree & a few gallons of water.—
Great Rice Eating & Song-Singing.—Turn in for a nap at 10'
and turn out for a nap at 12 o'clock of the night.—Indians.—
Morning. 12th Septembre. Fitzpatrick & Hatcher,—Hulan's adventure.—Signals of friendship, and the appearance of a war-
party of Cayquas in our Camp.—They thought us Texians or
Tejanos—They smoke, and Eat breakfast with us.—we accompany them to their village on a distant Creek.—Evening,—squaws
& papooses. Cabresses and Cowskins.—Hatcher is welcomed with
joy by the damsels among the Cayquas.—spotted ponies.—saddles & Stirrups.—Indian archery.—vermillion the rage—ventriloquism and Kioways—Calf Skins.—white wolf skins.—Indian war moccasins & ornamented bridles.—war coats.—Indian
dandy.—Spanish Captures,—Indian dogs & mules.—Our Camp.

The sun rose on the morning of the eleventh of Septembre, as
bright and warm as ever, and his cheering rays were welcomed
with pleasure by the little Company of explorers, whose camp had
been in the cool bottom, and who were now wending their way
up the hills, and along the hollows which connected with the main
prairie or plain. Like all the streams of this sandy and fragile
region, the south fork of the Canadian or the Rio Rojo (as I shall
hereafter for the sake of brevity choose to denominate it,) pursues
its course towards the East, between two immense barriers of
sand, gravel and rock, which, in some places, assume the character
of sloping but irregular hills or buttes, whilst in others they
mount to the heigth of four and five hundred feet perpendicular:
Such is the aspect of the Cañons of the Rio Rojo: places which
forbid all access to the waters of the River, and consequently
famous with all traders and explorers who find it necessary to
traverse this region. The Cañons however were already passed;
and we were at present about one hundred and eighty miles below

them: yet the main features of this eccentric river, were still preserved, and frequently after travelling a whole day's journey down its banks, unable to cross it by reason of its depth, ten chances out of 12, we passed its wide channel before dusk, as dryshod as the Isralites in their flight across the Red Sea. The sides of the stream, t'is true, were not So high and steep as the Cañons above, yet they often ascended to great heigths, and were in many places beyond all ascent or descent. Though these rugged barriers frequently closed in upon, and forbid all passage between their base and the river, yet in numerous places as we gradually approached the mouth, the hills receded and left small bottoms covered with cottonwood, grape-vines and sandburs. These bottoms, as might be supposed, were never of great extent: The course of the Rojo is too variable; alternately winding like a serpent from one side to the other & when elevated by freshets from its tributaries on the mountains, overrunning the whole basin. T'was in such a bottom, that our camp of last night had been pitched, and though the heat of the sun during the day had been excessive and a proportionate degree of coolness desirable, yet the searching breeze which blew over the river, and fanned us during the night, was anything but comfortable, and caused us to greet the sun with pleasure, as he peered over the Eastern plain, preparatory to starting on his daily journey. As we attained the summit of the hill, whence the prairie stretched out far and wide not unlike a boundless table, we cast a last look at the abandoned camping place below us, and beheld two "grain folk of the region" ride into it to discover what we had left and doubtlessly to appropriate the same. Their search proved unsatisfactory it appeared, for, finding nothing but an old ox, whom we had driven thus far from the mountains & who was now unable to travel further, they soon recrossed the river, and were seen gallopping over the plain, untill their forms had disappeared in the distance. After mounting the hills, and thus reaching the level plain, we pursued our course parallel to that of the river, occasionally where circumstances permitted, descending to its edge & travelling along its banks, untill impeded by the shifting barriers. Our route was unmarqued by any peculiarity, save now & then, a little valley covered with green growths of vines,—and hackberry bushes crossed our path, or some steep and insurmountable wall of crumbling mica and sand, appeared suddenly to cast itself suddenly before us. We likewise noticed numerous petrifications on the slopes of the hills, the first we had seen along this river, having the appearance of trees and stumps: Some of the tree-trunks, all of which were lying flat upon the ground, were 30 feet in length and 18 or 20 inches in diameter.[1]

The curious among us collected divers specimens of the same. The frequent chasms or rents in the borders of the river, which frequently descended to the depth of 4 & 500 feet, we passed, by descending to the river itself, and rounding their entrance or mouth, in order to save the distance which would be lost, by travelling around their head, frequently 6 or 8 miles distant from the river.

We journied along in this manner, untill noon, when a stop was suddenly put to our motions, by the interference of a stupendous wall or barrier of flint, several hundred feet high; the base of which was washed by the waves of the river, and whose sides were almost perpendicular. Here was a manifest dilemma: we had our choice; either to attempt the passage of the Rojo, and try our luck on its southern bank, or return to the main prairie by the way we came & travel around the head of the chasm. As the river, was, at this place, of more than usual depth, being more confined, and the prospect on the opposite shore looking very bleak and rugged, we were on the point of following the latter alternative when the

---

[1] Abert: "We noticed several trees in a state of petrifaction, which were covered with sparkling masses of clear rock crystal, and the ligneous fibre had in some places been supplied by pink-colored agate, which, shining through, gave to the whole a brilliant rosy hue, resembling rose quartz." *Guádal P'a*, 64.

118

attention of our band was directed to a suspicious looking group of out-landish horsemen, who appeared on the opposite heigths.

They discharged their fire arms, and uttered harmonious yells, when they beheld us, and forthwith began to descend the hill which sloped towards the river. We awaited their coming, and they most leisurely proceeded to seek a good fording place in order to cross over to our side.[2] They were but 8 or 10, and betokenend more boldness in thus riding into a camp of white men, than these prairie Indians generally do: The party of Camanches we met with above.—Buffaloe-Eaters by way of distinction, numbering double, showed great timidity, and whilst 2 or 3 of their seniors, rode into the camp, the balance remained at a distance, untill they saw that all was perfect friendship, & even then came only one after the other. These, on the contrary rode straight to us hailed us as brothers, shook hands, dismounted & sat down in a ring to have a talk. After being informed of our destination & our purpose in thus crossing their country, their chief, a merry faced, confident old fellow, whose whole body shook when he felt pleased, said he was much pleased to see his friends. (although he was a little puzzled to account for our extraordinary desire to explore his wild region.)[3] and that he could pilot us around the chasm in question by an easy route. As our friends appeared to be half-way suspicious of our designs, and every now & then cast an eye around at the mens' rifles, with a doubtful air, as much as to say, I'm plaguey sorry I've come here, for p'raps ye're Texan," and as we were desirous of being off, as soon as possible, The powow soon came to a close; a present of tobacco being first made our acquaintances. They were all Kiowas, save one & he was a

---

[2] Abert took security measures: "We motioned them to advance, at the same time choosing our position so as to be flanked by the river on one side, and a semicircular barrier of our wagons on the other. Into this 'kraal' we were securely placed whilst waiting the approach of friend or foe." *Ibid.*, 62.

[3] Abert notes the Indians' suspicion of a scientific expedition; they could not conceive a long journey as for any purpose other than trade or warfare. *Ibid.*, 61–62.

Mexican youth about 20. He was mounted & equipped like the balance, with spanish gun & bow. He was bareheaded—wore leggings and breech clout, and presented an admirable specimen of a renegade Mexican & a Kiowa brave. He was but one of the many, and I have beheld men 30 & 40 years of age,—boys from 12 to 20, and even women among these wild & barbarous Indians, who have been taken prisoner, and carried by their captors, far away from their native hamlets and their people, and have been transformed by time and circumstances into warriors and squaws as Indian-like as the Cayquas & Camanches themselves. T'is even reported in good authority, though I had no opportunity of testing its truth myself, that there are many American individuals thus circumstanced among the Camanches.[4]

By means of the manual signs which consitute the standard language, among all the prairie tribes, the old chief who engrossed the burden of conversation, informed us that nearly the whole of his village had gone down into Mexico. (For the humane purpose, no doubt, of easing the wretched Mexicans of a portion of their mules & horses), and that, by following the bed of the chasm or gorge, before us, for a short distance, we would reach a point, whence we might easily ascend to the prairie, on the opposite side of the said chasm or gorge. He, and his comrades soon left us, and we following, the intricacies of the tortuous ravine, over rocks and divers pits, finally arrived at a place where a gently sloping hill offered us a route to the plain above. By dint of much swearing & shouting and some pushing, we contrived to get our waggons to the summit, and not being any ways desirous of being again imprisoned among the rocks & hills, we struck off from the River, and pursued our route across the plain untill nearly sunset.

A ravine or gorge headed about 6 or 8 miles in the prairie:—

---

[4] Raids to capture prisoners for ransom or to be sold into slavery became a highly organized business in the Southwest. Carl Coke Rister, *Border Captives*; LeRoy R. and Ann W. Hafen, *The Old Spanish Trail*; L. R. Bailey, *Indian Slave Trade in the Southwest*.

at this place, a small quantity of rain water had collected in a curved rock—a couple of trees stood likewise there: This was our camp that night. The 2 trees constituted our supply of fuel. (There was not another tree to be seen within the bounds of the horizon.) and the rain-water in the rock supplied the material from which our handy cuiseniers composed an invigorating supply of coffee. This place was one of those, wherat there be not more fuel & water than will supply our camp & none to spare: So that, by the time each mess had gathered its fuel and drawn its water, there was but a scarcity left. The men were unusually cheerful and merry-hearted this evening, and many a joke & jovial tale went round, whilst the meal of dried meat & coffee was preparing. They seemed inspired by the beautiful moon, (a peerless one was floating in the clouds) to spin their wonderful yarns, for, untill a late hour, there were little knots or groups of Americans & Canadians, chatting & laughing around their respective fires. Our camp as was invariably the custom was pitched in the form of a circle, or rather of a square, the corners being occupied by the tents, whilst in the intervening spaces, the waggons were drawn up, so as to form a kind of enclosure or caral, as much for our own defence in case of an Indian attack, as for the security of our mules, which were, one & all securely picketed in the enclosed area. There were yet some, if I am not mistaken, still conversing at several of the messes, when the cry of "Turn out! Turn out!" shouted in the hoarse voice of the guard, aroused the sleeping camp, & occasioned a universal rush for guns & pistols and an issuing forth to combat the enemy.

In bold relief, between us & the clear sky, on the summit of a neighbouring butte of the prairie, stood a large party of mounted Indians.

They stood but for a moment however; for the alarm cry of the guard caused their dark figures to disappear as suddenly as they came. They were, beyond all doubt, pursuing our trail &

were following it with so much keenness, that in their haste, they had come upon our camp before they discovered their mistake. They were conversing in an audible voice when first seen on the swell, and involuntarily exposed their whole contour to the individuals of whom they were in quest. "How I'd like to try a bullet at them things" was a half-muttered wish of a comrade near me, as he cautiously took the cap from his gun, with the intention of again returning to his blankets. "No need for that Ben" observed another who noticed the act "you'll have use for that same cap 'fore day." The couple turned in for a nap,—the guards were relieved by fresh ones, and there being no immediate necessity for the whole camp to remain awake, in a short time, the members thereof were sound asleep "perfectly dead to glory" whilst the guards rubbed their heavy eyelids to discover through the gloom, (the moon was gone down) whether aught was about which bore the semblance of Indians. They saw nothing of the kind however, for morning came at last, and there was nothing yet discovered of our midnight visitors. "Tho" in the language of the drowsey guard, "some of the mules picketed near the Captain's tent did snort and fly 'round a little, and several break loose, thar war no Injuns about sure & sarten." The cooks were uncommonly smart this morning and the messes were breakfasting at an early hour. Our pilot and Hatcher (the hunter employed for 50 days at Bent's Fort), took their rifles, and sauntered over the surrounding swells, to discover if possible whether any of the visitors of the night were within hailing distance. Their search was, for some time, fruitless; our friends were unusually bashful, and if they were in the neighbourhood, they kept themselves quite close.

Finally as our 2 comrades were on the point of returning to camp, the pilot, being a man much experienced in such affaires, suddenly cast a look over the edge of the swell, he had just left; by which admirable and scientifick ruse-de-guerre, he obtained a momentary glimpse of one of our modest Red-Brethren, as he was intently engaged in observing the things "vot vent on in camp." A white signal was forthwith hoisted on our side, and waved to & fro, as a sign of friendship. A war-party of thirty or forty Cayquas, immediately rode out from behind the neighbouring buttes, and entered our camp, shaking hands as usual, & very much delighted to see us. "Nearly all their braves & warriers had gone down into Mexico.—(for the same purpose, doubtlessly, as the beforementioned braves),—Their village was about 8 or 10 miles distant on a small creek.—They had been roused by some Camanches (Old Foxes), who had seen us en route across the prairie & who had reported our numbers to exceed a thousand. (Camanches will lie.)—And that we were all Texians,—That we were invading their region.—The[y] also informed us that they had been following our trail and had come upon our camp most unexpectedly. (We were well aware of that.) They had been almost sure of our being Tejanos or Texians,—They didn't desire to injure Americans.—They had smoked a long time behind a butte, on the subject of running our animals off. (Our mules could scarcely walk, much less run,)—That they had come to the conclusion to first discover who we were. (we knew that too), and for this purpose, had despatched several of their most expert spies, after the moon was gone down, on a mission of espionage, for our benefit.—Also that these spies had approached, very near to our tents. (This explained why our mules flew round a little & some broke loose), one of them had crawled, within ten or twelve feet of Hatcher as he lay in the open air with several others near the edge of the ravine.—The spy aimed his Mexican shotgun at the sleeper,—at the same moment the latter arose on one elbow & exposed his features in the firelight.—The Indian thought he remembered the physiognomy, and drew back his gun. (Hatcher, by the way, is Bent's trader among the Cayquas & Camanches.)

His heart told him that it was wrong to shoot, for the man was not a Texian but an American.[5]—He, and his comrades forthwith descended into the ravine and returned unperceived to their comrades, resolving to see more of the strangers."

Such was the substance of their statements; we we[re] half-inclined to disbelieve the greater portion, particularly the latter, but when we considered within ourselves, how probable it might be that the guard was half asleep, and how easy such a manoeuvre as that which the Indians claimed to have accomplished, could have been executed. (The ravine with its rocks and hollows afforded excellent concealment.)—When we looked upon the main hero of the exploit,—a finely featured Indian of good mould & stature, and whose look bespoke a greater portion of intelligence than usually falls to the majority of Cayquas, and above all, when this warrior pointed to a little pyramid of stones erected by him, during his midnight visit, at the edge of the rock, as a proof to support his assertions, we felt ourselves convinced, and several habitually incredulous shrugged their shoulders as if almost convinced likewise. All being thus explained and the entire misunderstanding made up, The Red braves were invited to breakfast & a smoke of paper cigars. A present of tobacco was also made. Though it be rather impolite and smack much of bad-manners, [to criticize] guests whom you invite to your board, I cannot refrain from mentioning here, the existence of a certain fashion among these same people, which be not only novel and original, but is, at the same time so handy as would almost excite the envy of the polite Count D'Orsay himself.[6] Though the genteel Frenchman gives good and clear directions in his book, how a gentlemen or lady, should hold the knife & fork, as also how such & such

[5] Abert says that Hatcher and the Indian "by daylight . . . recognized each other and heartily shook hands." *Guádal P'a*, 66.

[6] Alfred Guillaume Gabriel de Grimod, Comte d'Orsay (1801–52), a French adventurer and dandy who married into the family of the Earl of Blessington and set himself up in London as man of fashion, arbiter of taste, gambler, and sportsman.

things should be done, yet these anti-fashion,—anti-Count D'Orsay Cayquas not only, pay no regard at all to what either directs, but in defiance of all kinds of manners, disdain to use either knife or fork, scientifically making use instead thereof, of all their thumbs and fingers. (I had almost added toes.) They be likewise much opposed to the luxury of plates, and when, as on the 12th of Sept 1845, a party of Kiowas sit down to table, each individual appropriates a separate dish. One for example, takes the dish of bread,—another seizes upon the meat tray, whilst a third takes possession of the entire plate of molasses & rice: each one esteeming it his duty to demolish everything in the dish before him.

This state of affairs was but a sorry fulfillment of the fearful prophecy of one, who, during the last night's confusion, in camp, gave it, as his serious opinion, that "We'd have a smart chance of scrimmage 'fore morning, and thar mout be a few killed & then thar moutn't be none." Yet it was well enough that things turned out as they did, for, had the guard not been asleep,—had he discovered the lurking savages, and had he pierced the pericranium of the spy, as the latter peered at the sleepers over the edge of the rock,—the inevitable consequences would have been, (so argued a learned one), that the comrades of the deceased would have been enraged by the act, and would have considered it their duty to avenge his death.—The whole Kiowa nation would then become excited against us,—Their allies, the Camanches would consequently have been excited too, and we, poor devils,—but 35 in number, would have had to fight our way, through the whole posse, in order to reach the settlements; all merely on account of one dead Cayqua. Eu! Euge![7] Thus did kind fate ordain, that no guard was entirely awake,—that the spy wasn't seen,—and that of course he wasn't shot and therefore that we would have no Cayquas and Camanches to fight through to reach our homes.

[7] "Good! Well done!" Montaignes is airing his Greek.

Bravo! All was friendly,—all was sociable. The gentlemanly warriors, instead of seeking our lives, offered their services to conduct us to their village, about half-a-day's journey in a distant creek, whence, they informed us we could approach the Rio Rojo in such a manner as to profit a whole day's travel. We had no objections to this, and saddling up our mules, we rode along in company with our kind acquaintances, chatting & spinning yarns with them with great volubility, and with exceeding amusement, could the one have understood one particle of what the other was talking about.

The Indians were all admirably mounted, and evinced considerable horsemanship. There were among them several youths of 16 or 18 years, yet these were rigged off with shield bow lance & gun, and as they galloped over the plain, in mock pursuit of a curious antelope who had approached us,—their long hair and lenthy fringes, mixing with the glossy mane & tail of their steeds, & floating in the wind, gave them the appearance of Mercuries mounted on Pegasi. Several there were among them, who were habited in war-coats or short buckskin jackets without sleeves, covered profusely with feathers and variously coloured beads.— Others again wore long queues made of the long hair of the buffaloe joined to their own, these were of great length,—sometimes extending to their heels,—plaited & greased with great nicety, and ornamented with different sized plates of silver and brass, the largest being nearest the head, and diminishing towards the extremity.

After passing over a more uneven country than was usually to be found at this distance from the river, composed principally of various coloured flint, we arrived about 11 o'clock at a small creek which was nearly dry: whatever water there was in it, being collected in holes or small ponds in its channel. Here we encamped: being about one mile below the village of the Cayquas.

Several old squaws and children, came to our camp soon after our arrival and by the time our dinner was finished, nearly the whole Cayqua village was with us.

All brought something wherewith to trade, for these people, consider every stranger passing through their country, as a person coming for no other purpose but to trade. We had a sorry assortment of articles to traffick with them, and a wretched lot of old unchewable & unsmokable tobacco which Capt Frémont had kindly supplied us with at Bent's Fort, constituted the principal exchange of today, in return for the ropes & cowskin, which they brought.

These Indians are great archers & several of the boys, who thronged our camp, & who appeared no larger than nine pins, shewed scientific marksmanship and adroitness, & striking buttons with their arrows, 20 steps distant. They shot the buttons with great dexterity & when a few beads and tobacco was put up to be shot for, they evinced greater.

The greatest demand on the part of our red customers was for vermillion. There was but little of this amongst us, and this when received by the squaws was bountifully bestowed upon the swarthy physiognomies of their numerous progeny which pressed around for a sufficiency & when supplied, strutted around in infantile pride, feeling no doubt far grander than so many nabobs.

Dandyism prevails to a great extent among the youth of this tribe, as well as among most of the other nations of aboriginees, and numerous braves, with ornamented cues & leggings, strutted about our tents, looking as if desirous to be admired & not to admire.

The dogs, of which there are great numbe[rs] among these Kiowas, look most uncanine and have more the exterior of a wolf than that of the domestic quadruped, by whose name they are called.

The savages returned to their lodges at sunset, & left us to sup and sleep in quietness, in order to be prepared for the morrow's journey.

Several Spanish youths, prisoners among these Cayquas, were noticed by us, clothed or rather naked like the Indians, & galloping around on horseback, like actual bedouins of the desert.[8]

CHAPTER FOURTEEN

Wolves—Mexicans and Kioways.

Mᴏʀᴇ Indian visiters. — our start.—The Cayqua procession.—description of their village.—our route.—Camp.—3 Indians.—Wolf-who-looks-over-the hill.—his exploit in Mexico.—The Crow Squaw.—Hank & hackberries.—The Indian's oration at 9. P.M.—Indian hieroglyphics.—small dog. The 14th.—Indian dog serenade from the hill-tops.—grape vines.—The 3 Indians accompany us as guides.—Pather's second race and the gallantry of the Crow Squaw.—The Bluffs.—Crossing.—ducking.—cold water & grapes—turkies.—The 15th.—The soil.—roadmaking.—plums.—Spaniards.—A Pueblo Indian.—trader looking for old Bald-Head.—our camp.—approach of a party of Cayquas.—a horse swap.—departure of Hatcher & Greenwood.—The 16th.—leave Red River.—cross Kiowa Creek.—Camp on Arrow Creek.—A tremendous Bear tale.—The 17th. Fanny Squears.—Leave Arrow Creek.—antelope—a flag hoisted.—2 Buffaloe Bulls.—no water—Elk Creek.

---

[8] Abert comments that these youths "being well treated, were perfectly content with their new situation; they said that they were in fact better situated than in their own country, for they had plenty to eat, and were more kindly treated than in the place whence they had been taken." *Guádal P'a,* 67.

—fresh tracks of Savages.—Dewey sees 3 Indian warriors afar off.—Night.—a Shout from the guard at 11 O'Clock.—Camp turns out and the spies run away.—The 18th.—Indians.—an Elk Skin coat of mail.—Bridles & horses.—our route.—Camp on Elk Creek a 2nd time.—a Somersault extraordinaire.—arrival of Indian Squaws and a mujer Españole.—Nabajo Blankets.—a squaw in mourning.—Belanger's dilemma.—Muskeet.—Little-wolf.—our departure.—5 miles travel.—Camp again on Elk Creek.—The 19th.—sandy bottoms and sandy hills—Scrub oak —acorns.—the mouth of Cutnose Creek—Plaster of paris.—The River becomes dry—Travel till 2 PM.—Our Camp.—

The morning following our arrival at this barbarian village (the 13th), the prairie around us was soon enlivened with troops of playful ponies of divers hues, though by far the prevailing was spotted, which sported around our band of travel-worn animals, as if desirous to persuade them to a frolic and a refreshing chase among the cool hills. Our Cavajarde however was proof against their wily manouevres, and our steady old Mexicanos and Californicos merely condescended to raise their sagacious heads, and cast an inquisitive glance at their wild visiters, as much as to say, "You can't come that game over me, mister Indian, and if you are frolicksome, it's no reason that I should be: for I have many miles to travel yet."

A few ungovernable and fractious mules who seemed envious of the idle lot of the ponies, took the occasion to make an inconsiderate move towards the hills, but were soon brought back. Now & then the tall form of a warrior as he strode over the hills to look for his steeds, envellopped in his long black blanket of Mexico, whilst a frequent form of less dimensions, clothed in the gaudy blue & pink Nabajoe blanket, marked a Cayqua squaw. After our early meal, our Caravan started from this place, & ascending the hills, which commanded a prospect of the Indian village with its lodges and people, we proceeded at our usual pace, for 6 hours over a succession of heavy and broken swells, or abrupt waves of the prairie. As we cast our eye towards the Kioway village below us, we could perceive the lodge of its chief or of its medicine, I do not know. Rings of red were drawn around its outside, as a mark of distinction, and the balance of the tents or lodges of which there were two score, were pitched in the form of a circle. A good spring of cold and clear water, gushed out near this village, from one of the banks of the ravine, and as we gradually increased the distance between us & our camping place of the night, we beheld the entire population of this barbaric town, winding along the hills, in Indian file, one after the other, warrior, boy, squaw & girl, from our camp towards their homes, whilst many a diminutive papoose, mounted on a fleet courser, without a saddle, & with no bridle but a hair rope, scouring like a thing of air, across the surrounding swells of the region.

We reached a creek of good size towards one o'clock, & crossed it thrice, before we pitched our camp, its valley was about a mile in width, and the channel of the river itself, occupied about 100 yards. Its bed was of sand, & the water was scarcely flowing, but as we proceeded along its banks, its depth increased. The groves along it were principally composed of cottonwood, hackberry, willow & vines. It flowed East, and we encamped on its southern bank, in a thick little grove of hackberry about, 3 o'clock P.M.

About 4 o'clock, 3 Indians, 2 men & a Crow squaw, joined our camp. Whereof one, a Cayqua, sporting the title of Wolf-who-looks-over-the hill was a veritable barbarian warrior and was our guide in future, as far as the old trading station whitherto we were travelling. He was mounted on an extraordinary mule of Mexican extraction, with which according to Wolf's own account, he had successfully pursued many a buffaloe on the plains.—he had vermillion on his face, brass wire wrapped many times around his brawny wrists, & with his ornamented queue, his Spanish bridle, his leggings,—his fantastic stirrups, his Mexican gun and his bows and arrows, he looked the beau ideal of an American Bedouin of the Rio Rojo.[1]

The other man was of middle age apparently and had pre-possessing features,—his high forehead well shaped nose, and modest exterior for an Indian, had a good effect upon the white men. After dark, our wolfish friend, went out several rods from the camp, and in a clear, sonorous voice, bade all lurking Indians who might have been prowling about, in the language of his country, to remain where they were, untill morning. This was for the purpose not only of informing them that we were friends, but, under the supposition of there being any Camanches among them, of keeping them at a distance, untill daylight should explain their design & numbers. The pitchy darkness of the night, relieved only at the several fires of the messes, around which stood the groups of Americans & Canadians conversing in their usual jocose man-ner and the voice of the eloquent warrior, speaking to his people, had a most picturesque effect & would, if voice could be imparted to the canvas have afforded Salvator Rosa, a subject for his magic pencil.[2]

The night passed without any disturbance, and on the morn (the 14th), we were roused from our slumbers, by the quick, sharp bark of several Indian dogs, serenading us from the hill-tops. Their bark resembles that of the prairie wolf, and favours the opinion of these animals being connected. One of them, a small, straight eared black cur, soon entered the camp, & recog-nised his lord.

---

[1] Abert gives the guide's name as Tish-na-zi, "a man of a very happy disposition" who "amused us as he sprang around while constructing his rude shelter for the night and repeating the words 'how d'ye do,' 'yet,' in playful mimicry of the whites. These few words were all he could remember of the English language, except a few profane oaths." *Guádal P'a,* 68.

[2] Salvator Rosa (1615–73), Italian painter, etcher, poet, actor, and musician. As romantic artist he appealed to the nineteenth century. His landscapes were savage scenes peopled with shepherds, seamen, or soldiers; he was notable for battle art.

We continued down the stream which flows into the fork on the north, and proceeded through sandy bottoms covered with dense thickets of grape vines & hackberry, untill the interference of a stupendous bluff which overhung the river, impeded our passage & compelled us to cross the stream. Several groups or scattered piles of lodge poles and boughs, as also several circular indentations in the ground, wherein, hides had been smoked or boucaned[3] marqued the remnants of abandoned villages.

Patrick's mule (Pate), being of a most erratic disposition, and being left alone by his master for a second, esteemed it his priviledge to make the best use of his time, & forthwith made off, at a distance from the balance of the cavejarde, & for some time eluded all efforts on Patrick's part, to catch him. The Crow squaw, mounted on her palfry, which by the way was nothing less than a Mexican mule, forthwith volunteered her services to catch the recreant Pate, & with great address & more gallantry kindly waylaid said Pate, and handed him over to the further direction of his lord & master Patrick. After crossing the stream, which was 3 & in some places 4 feet deep, we pursued our route for a few miles along the other bank and came in sight of the embouchure of our stream into the Red River. We encamped at the foot of the bluffs, and found cold water within a few hundred yards. 3 wild turkies were shot by Hatcher. Other game was scarce. Our Cayqua guide here repeated his loud incantations of last night to the dark manes who might have been around us in the hollows & among the rocks, and we experienced no difficulty from any of these latter, that night. At Sunrise, we left this camp and wended our way over rough ridges of rock and red sand and passing the feet of several steep bluffs composed of a species of plaster and frequently of mica, were forced again to dismount and use the pick and shovel. We passed along a road or path, which was confined between the

[3] The French *boucaner*, meaning to smoke meat on a wooden frame. Buccaneer derives from this word because pirates of the West Indies barbecued cattle along the beaches.

bluff and the edge of the river and after several hundred yards passed in this way, finally attained the summit of a hill, from whose top descended a slope into the river bottom. Several objects had been perceived on the upland, which were supposed to be Indians; But our Indian pilot; Wolf who looks-over-the-hill, had rode out upon the prairie, and the objects turned out to be a party of Mexican traders and several pueblo Indians, who were seeking, the band of Camanches under old Bald Head, for the purpose of traffic.

When the party, beheld the form of our Cayqua on his mule, scouring over the prairie towards them, they beat their mules and attempted an escape. He however, to humour their sport, gave the war yell and was rapidly gaining, upon them. They soon found out their mistake and Wolf found his squaw in the group. We soon afterwards saw one of the Spaniards at a distance, standing, as if loath to come to us, whilst 2 of their company, Pueblo Indians, came up to us in a most confident manner.[4] These Pueblos or Christian Indians, talk a mongrel Spanish, and are generally more miserable than any other Indians. Such is the effects of a perverted form of Christian missionism. Travelling along the valley, for 6 or 8 miles, through large sandbeds, and fields of tall & wavy grass we finally pitched our camp on the south side of the Rio Rojo, one mile distant from its water, and about three above the point whereat formerly stood the trading post of which we were in search.[5]

[4] Abert describes the Pueblo Indians: "They were dressed in conical-crowned sombreros, jackets with the stripes running transversely; large, big breeches extending to the knees; long stockings and moccasins. They were badly armed, and presented a shabby and poor appearance, though we learned that they were a good specimen of the class to which they belong." *Guádal P'a,* 71.

[5] A trading post established in the winter of 1843–44 on Bent's Creek in northeastern Hutchinson County. Hatcher and Greenwood left the party here to return to Bent's Fort. Abert says of Hatcher: "It was with much regret that we saw him depart. He had, by his gentlemanly deportment, won upon the regard of all; whilst, by his knowledge of the people and country, he had rendered much valuable service in our intercourse with the Indians." *Ibid.,* 72, note 203.

There was but little fuel to be found, and we expected to have a long distance to bring our water, had not a cool spring been discovered among the bluffs. Wolf-who-looks-over-the-hill ascended one of the buttes, and discharged his gun several times in the air. A party of 8 or ten Cayqua warriors soon crossed the river and came to the camp. One of our horses was exchanged to one of them for another, and our visiters departed that night, accompanied by Hatcher & Greenwood, whose journey was here at an end, and who were now to return across the country to Bent's Fort, whence they had accompanied us. A storm was apparently threatening, the clouds were blowing to & fro, & the air was gradually darkened. We felt, quite sad at the departure of our friends, & our hearts felt no lighter, when we thought of the dangers to which they would be exposed. Savages,—thirst,—hunger & weather. "We travel by night, & we lay by during the day" they said, & shaking hands, they rode away with our red warriors, whose forms after they forded the distant river, gradually lessened untill they disappeared towards the West.

Our pilot, the Crow squaw & her man were also parted with at this place, and as we started on our march, the following morning (16th) & struck off in a southern direction, almost at right angles with the river, their absence was very sensibly felt. We crossed Kiowa Creek to Arrow Creek.[6] Here was a seepe of water, where that element exuded from the sandy bed of the creek. We encamped in a grove of hackberries and cottonwood for the night. Towards the close of the day, as Walter Harden, strolled carelessly along the side of the stream, seeking for grapes, among the thickets of the vine which lined its edge, a fearful growl from a clump of hackberries a few yards before him, caused him to wheel most suddenly, and run with exceeding celerity to the opposite

---

[6] Arrow Creek is identified as White Deer Creek, east of Alhambra, Texas, by H. Bailey Carroll. Abert describes it as "a fine stream of pure water, remarkably straight, and well timbered with characteristic cottonwood, and lined along its bank with excellent pasturage." *Ibid.*, 73, note 206.

side of the creek. Here, he turned about, & with a face blanched with terror, gazed earnestly at the thicket, where the terrific growl had proceeded. Another heart-appalling Boo! came from the hackberries and Walter was just starting, to camp, when the head of François peered over the bushes & asked what he was in such a hurry for.

On the 17th, we hitched up our animals and made an early start from, this dry looking creek which is known as Arrow Creek, and ascending to the plain, pursued our route across it beneath a burning sun, whose hot rays glanced from the overheated plain and blinded our eyes to all that was before us, untill we attained the edge of a dry creek, whose bed was covered with sharp gravel. Pursuing our way down its bed for several hundred yards, a seepe of water was at last discovered under the right bank and our camp was forthwith pitched on the border. We had seen antelope during the day, and several old bulls, were lazily cropping the burnt herbage in the distance. Several of our men attempted to approach them, but the wind was unfavorable and the buffaloe escaped. The dancing rays of heat reflecting from the plain, frequently deceived us, and the unusual appearance of some[thing] tall seen through them, influenced us with the idea of Indians, and so much so, that our banner, a white mosquito bar, was reared & waved aloft upon a tent pole & borne in advance of the caravan, in order to inform all strangers around of our pacific intention.

Throughout this day's journey, water was not to be found, & when we at length arrived at the dry creek, I have mentioned, which bears the name of Buffaloe Creek, and is more properly the main False Ouachita, it was as much as we could do to prevent our unruly animals from spoiling the scanty supply of water, into which they rushed to allay their thirst.[7]

[7] Abert writes that the sun was intensely hot. The prairie stretched flat in every direction with nothing to break the monotony. The men became gloomy and despondent. "The idea of having been misled evidently began to steal into our minds. . . . tales we had heard . . . of treachery, surprise, and massacre were

To strengthen our opinion concerning the proximity of Indians, Mr. Stephen Cooper[8] related having seen several tracks of moccasin and mules in the sandy bed, which appeared of recent make. Towards sunset also Oliver Dewey, strolled forth among the buttes, in search of curiosities more than game, and during this hunt, beheld several miles distant, 3 Indian warriors, their snow-white shields shining in the last rays of the sun. He fired his gun, & made signals for them to come towards him, but they disappeared among the buttes.

Night came, & a strong guard was placed around the camp.—Every man was advised to be on his guard against surprise, and we slept with our rifles in our hands.

This was not useless, for about midnight the alarm cry of Harden the guard, roused us from our slumbers, and caused an unusual stir among several Indians, who were lurking in the grass, which fringed the river, & whom, Harden's shout, caused to start from their places of concealment & escape with speed, through the scattered groves.

The mule guards for the next morning whilst watching their charge, to prevent their wandering, beheld several black objects having the appearance, in the distance of wild turkies, moving along the edge of a butte on the opposite side of the creek.

One of the men, more suspicious than the other immediately raised the alarm of Indians. Mr. Fitzpatrick hoisted our flag,—the same old mosquito [bar,]—and waving it towards the butte on which the objects had been seen, cried out in Spanish. "Americano! Americano!" 12 or 14 mounted warriors forthwith pre-

---

evidently revolving in our minds. This sort of depression, akin to fear, is contagious; and as we pursued our way each one examined his rifle, and closed in with the main body." Late in the afternoon the terrain changed and as a long line of bluffs was seen on the horizon, forebodings disappeared. By the time they reached camp all were lighthearted and gay. *Journal*, 49.

[8] Stephen Cooper, named in Abert's list of men on the expedition, seems not to have been related to Isaac Cooper.

sented themselves upon the butte, & cried out ["]Kiowah! Kiowah! ["]

One of our men shouted forth to the strength of his lungs, "Amojo! Amijos!" A wag added in a voice as loud, ["]Muchos! Bravos! ["]

The camp was convulsed with laughter which was not in the least diminished by the entry of our wild friends.

They rode up to the tent of our chief, as usual, and loosing their steeds to enjoy the pasturage, placed themselves in a circle upon the grass to talk & smoke with the white men.

Those who had been detected in their nocturnal approach towards our camp last night, recognised Harden as the one whose vigilance had defeated their designs. They had, with the quick eyes of Indians, remembered well the features of the guard as he sat in the light of the fire. These Indians had several elegant horses.—They had spears ten or 12 feet in length,—shields,— bow & arrows, & several had short Mexican guns. They were accoutred like the Indians we had seen before, but appeared to be a more sensible set. Although one old fellow, among them having over his shoulders, a well-dressed elkskin, shrugged his shoulders, when pressed by us to exchange it for something else, and gave as his reason, that it was proof against bullets, & no Texian could shoot through it. After smoking and breakfasting our new acquaintances mounted their steeds & accompanied us in our route down the creek for 2 hours.—We again camped on this Buffaloe Creek after going 6 miles, and there awaited the arrival of the Kiowa village, who, as we were informed were among the hills near the horizon. Just before we encamped, whilst crossing the bed of the stream which was here flowing, my little mule placed her forefeet down the bank, & remained in that position, untill my saddle & myself slipped over her head.

We had no more than pitched our tents, than a number of Kiowa squaws, with a mujer español or Spanish woman of beauty,

137

riding with them, entered our camp. They brought ropes & robes to trade, but we had nothing to exchange except tobacco. Several of these squaws had Nabajo blankets around them. One of them had her face gashed, & the blood oozing from the wounds covered her face & was permitted to dry in that position. Such I was informed was the Cayqua mode of mourning for a deceased relation.

These Kiowa squaws are a weather beaten set, and it would have made you laugh, to see the dilemma, in which Belanger was placed, by a hideous old squaw, who clasped him in her arms & called him her recreant son: she had lost one some 20 years ago. We were all sunburnt very much & the old damsel cannot be blamed for mistaking our Canadian for a Cayqua. They likewise brought with them, amongst other things, a kind of sweetmeat consisting of pulverized seeds of a dwarf locust, called by them Muskeet.[9] The powder has a sweetish taste and resembles in that respect the glutinous pod or covering of the honeylocust pea.

Taking leave of this village, we travelled about 5 miles & again encamped on Buffalo Creek.—Wood was scarce, and drift wood was our principal fuel. We were in motion at an early hour on the 19th, and pursuing our route through numerous sandy bottoms, along the creek, we soon reached a portion of country, whose appearance brought to our minds the looks of our own brush prairies at home. The country was gently rolling,—it was extremely sandy—and over the whole surface for a couple of miles distant from the edge of the creek, extended a dense little forest of dwarf oaks, not more than 2 feet in heigth.[10]

They were very productive of acorns, & the ground beneath

[9] Mesquite.

[10] Abert calls these dwarf oaks "shin oaks." The shin oak grows in scattered clumps in sandy lands in southeastern New Mexico and Texas, occasionally in great thickets, known to frontiersmen as "shinneries," where the tree has been known to reach four feet or more. Normally the shin oak seldom grows higher than two feet. *Guádal P'a*, 85.

them was covered with large quantities of goodly sized nuts of agreable flavour. Whilst travelling along, we beheld the mouth or entrance of Cut-nose Creek which enters Buffaloe from the south. The region on the opposite side, was very desolate, and had a barren & most Sahara like aspect.

Passing many huge masses of plaster and micacous limestone,[11] we finally attained a point in the river, where it was completely dry.—At 2 P.M. we pitched our camp on its banks, at a point where an inconsiderable rivulet came in on the North.

[11] Micaceous, or mica-bearing, limestone is rare, but micaceous sandstone abounds in the area Montaignes describes.

CHAPTER FIFTEEN

The 20th.—Sandburrs—Camp for the last time on Buffaloe—The False Ouachita.—The Great Pawnee War-Ground. The 21st.—Leave Buffaloe Creek.—groves of timber.—Camp.—wild turkies.—a spring—The 22nd.—a small stream.—a Camanche Encampment.—a horseguard asleep. —The 23rd.—Follow the creek—Bands of Buffaloes.—wild Turkies.—The great Buffaloe surround by Cooper.[1]—Jamieson. —Hulan—Mint—Vachand.—We camp on a small Fork.—a word respecting the Pawnees or Panis.—The 24th.—strike Red River.—a Mexican Panther—a Buffaloe Bull bemired.—a difficult access to water.—25th—dry channel of Red River,—cross creeks & hills.—noon at a hole—ducks.—antelope—camp.— Harden kills a Bull & 3 deers—a Bear Serenade—The 26th— Buffaloe in every direction.—tetras utraphrosianus.—a small

[1] Isaac Cooper or Stephen Cooper? Montaignes probably means himself.

creek.—old Indian encampment.—good water.—Harden and Yunt cross the River in search of Buffaloe.—Rauchon & Rivon do the same.—mule mired.—Old Beaver dam.—La Tulippe's pet beaver & his adventure on the Riviere Grosse Corne with Beaver & Blackfeet.—The Pawnees again—The return of the hunters— Their success.—packs of wolves.—a kind of hard plaster.—

On the 20th & 21st we continued our course along Buffaloe Creek, passing for the most part over a country covered with the scrub or dwarf oak which I have mentioned, occasionaly crossing some little bottom covered with sandburs—and confined by some huge bluff of plaster; On the 20th, we camped about 12 o'clock and though at this place there was not a drop of water in the wide channel, we succeeded in finding some at a little spring or seepe. We were now in the region known as the Great Pawnee War Ground, and on the following morning the 21st, we struck off from this creek which now turned its direction to a directly southern course, and travelled in a North Eastern direction untill 2, o'clock. The aspect of the country was generally level & covered with scrub oak, & after leaving these, the level prairie was spotted here & there with hundreds of little groves, of oak & hackberry, crowded with flocks of wild turkies. Finding a spring of water about 2 o'clock, we encamped at one of these groves. Whilst some employed themselves in mending the fractured waggon, others went forth in quest of turkies. Both were successful. The waggon or carriage was supplied with a tongue, & the messes with turkies. The 22nd beheld our encampment on a romantic little rivulet about 20 miles distant, and near by where a vast encampment of Cayquas or Camanches had formerly been; The brush & bushes which formed the skeltons of their tents being yet standing. At this place Duncan Linn was discharged for suffering himself to lie down by the rivulet & fall asleep, whilst he should have kept his eyes open & guarded the mules. He was much perplexed when he awoke from his nap, at discovering the absence of his gun, which he had by him when awake & which Mr. Fitzpatrick had carried off in the meanwhile.

On the 23rd, following the course of the little rivulet, and crossing it in several places, we at length ascended to the high prairie which formed the dividing ridge between the main Red River and the south fork of the Canadian. As we crossed the hollows or gaps which frequently furrowed the prairie, we scared up several wild turkies, & as we wound over the level numerous bands of buffaloe presented themselves in the distance. About 11 o'clock a large band of these animals, getting the wind of us, became terrified and mistaking our caravan; for a troupe of their own species, immediately gallopped towards us. Several of our wise ones, amongst whom was old Jamieson slid from their saddles, & with their rifles in their hands, ran across the plain, in order to intercept the buffaloe, as they attempted to pass. Old Jamieson had run with the rest for several hundred yards, but in the ardour of the chase, had cast not a single glance towards the prey. He kept his body bent towards the ground as he ran, in order not to alarm the buffaloe which he expected would rush over him each moment. Our boys shouted to him to lie down & not scare the buffaloe for they were coming.—Old Jamieson laid down upon the grass as far as his great quantum of paunch would allow, and as the boys still yelled forth to him to lie closer, he made frequent attempts to insert his capacious corpse into the unyielding soil. He remained in this posture several moments, not daring to raise his head an inch above its position for fear of scaring the approaching game, and when he finally did elevate it, it was but to discover that the herd of buffaloe was a mile distant, & that the wags were but making a butt of him.

This was not all the joke: poor Jamieson as well as his companions were ordered to trip it on their light gum elastic feet for the balance of the day.

141

We camped this night on a small fork.

Buffaloe bulls were seen in great numbers the next day, and when we camped at evening within 2 miles of the Rio Rojo, on a deep ploughed little rivulet, where water was difficult to be got at, we found in its miry bed a veteran bull, firmly secured in its slough. A large panther was likewise aroused by us from this place, & made a most picturesque appearance, as he made his retreat over the neighbouring hills.

The following day, (the 25th) we reached the banks of the South Fork, and found a wide but extremely dry channel. Travelling along, sometimes in its channel at others, along its rough banks scarred with numerous gaps, we reached about 12 o'clock a small hole in the side of the bed, in which was a quantity of poor water. Here we nooned. We again geared & saddled our animals after they became a little rested, and continued our rough passage along the southern bank. It was extremely broken & many little holes of water, were in the deep seams or ravines. At one of these were a number of shitepokes & several ducks one of which was brought down in its airy flight by our scientific leader. We likewise saw among the abrupt hills, several flocks of antelope and as many wolves. We camped on a little creek, and procured water from the holes into which it had settled in its sandy bed.

Towards dusk Walter Harden brought down a large bull,[2] & still later killed 3 deer. 2 does & a faun; 2 of which were brought into camp & found to be extraordinary poor.

The faun was brought in or rather nigh our camp about midnight by a tremendous bear, whose ravenous & terrific cries as he devoured it filled the guard with unpleasant association.

This Bear Encampment was left at the usual hour the following morning and we travelled over the prairie at a swift rate descending hills & ascending others, & then sweeping over a level of 5 or

[2] This bull, killed a mile from camp, was the largest yet seen by the expedition. Abert went out to sketch it and returned with the scalp, which was covered with hair thirteen inches long. *Guádal P'a*, 91.

6 miles extent, covered with numerous bands of buffaloe, who ran in every direction as we approached, whilst now and then a coqde-prairie (tetras europhasianum). Many balls whistled among these bands of buffaloe as they wheeled closely around us, but the shots, being discharged at random took no certain effect. About 2 o'clock the appearance of many bushes and lodge poles scattered around indicated the presence of a camping place, and we forthwith pitched our tents on a small dry branch which, when flowing, empties into the Rojo. The channel of the latter at this place was upwards of a mile in width, and over the whole of this space, there was flowing but a small quantity of water in the southern side, not deeper than 2 or 3 inches. Ancient beaver cuttings were noticed in the little creek and on the opposite hills of the river fed several bands of buffaloe. Harden & Yunt, Revar and Rouchon took their rifles & crossed in pursuit of these, whilst the balance of us sat around our fire of dry lodge poles & listened to the words of old La Tulippe who appeared to regain all his youthful ardor & spirit of merriment from the appearance of the beaver cuttings he had seen.

"Yase, you laugh, but laugh more. La Tulippe know damn well all bout bièvre & Black feet too. Ah, oui. les pieds noirs.—rascales —damn rascales for steal hoss and kill Franchman.["]

"But they never killed you La Tulippe."

"C'est vrai, it not their fault anyhow. The damned rascales look for me many time & once man year go, on the Big Horn the Grosse Corne, parmi les montaignes, these rascal Blackfeet come on 4 of us, who were fix traps in the Riviere.—Hee Hee Heeheeh, —they shoot arrows & yell. They kill les autres mais pour moi, I drop my trap & run like one deer over the rocks. They on horseback & cant follow vite, So I run & run & lose my hat. I keep on long time. The damn rascales! At last I get much fatigue and hide myself sans chapeau & sans moccasins on a leetle creek, leetle one. Here I stay till night, fear of the villain Blackfeet. Bout midnight, as I lay down on the grass by the creek, I fall sleep. Damn fatigue I tell. All at once I hear one grand splash in the wate, another one tap tap tap. Eheh! Pardieu, you no catch me. I jump up like one deer. I leave my moccasins & I run up the bank ver quick. No more splash in the wate. I wait when I get on the bank & squat down on the rock, for see wat dat which splash in the wate peut-être ce sont. Blackfeet, I think. I lay on de rock till daylight. Pardieu dere was one grand Bievre dam, in de creek, & the Bievres were driving the stakes in the ground with their tails.["]

This eccentric individual, this La Tulippe was a hard used veteran of the mountains, & had doubtlessly beheld many a skirmish and hard fought fight in that debateable ground of the aboriginees. He was adorned with numerous scars like every war worn hero, but no history save his own lips, informed mankind of his adventures. Knowing his authority to be respectable in such affairs, I enquired of him, concerning the truth of the circumstance narrated by many writers who inform us that the Pawnees have a custom of sacrificing human victims to the great Star.[3] Selon La Tulippe the Pawnees rub human fat or grease over all their weapons of war & hunting & over different implements used in husbandry. This they say secures success in fight and chase and insures a splendid crop to the labours performed in the field by their labourious squaws.

The men who had crossed the river in pursuit of buffaloe, returned at dusk, and reported, 2 Buffaloe killed: a cow and a calf. It was late & they did not return for the meat.[4] Large packs of

---

[3] Sacrifice of a young maiden, usually a captive, to the Great or Morning Star by the Skidi Pawnees was one of the rare instances of human sacrifice by Indians north of Mexico. The annual spring ceremony seems to have declined after 1818, with the last known instance occurring in 1838. Ralph Linton, *The Sacrifice to the Morning Star by the Skidi Pawnee*; George Amos Dorsey, *Traditions of the Skidi Pawnee*; George E. Hyde, *Pawnee Indians*; Katharine C. Turner, *Red Men Calling on the Great White Father*, 45–58.

[4] Abert concurs: "As it was late, and the meat some distance from camp, we preferred leaving it to wolves rather than risk men and mules out of camp after dark." *Guádal P'a*, 91.

wolves were noticed promenading in the sandy bed of the river, today, mostly of that tall grey kind called the common Grey Wolf. A kind of hard white plaster was also picked up by the curious, & manufactured into neat pipes by the ingenious.

CHAPTER SIXTEEN

Which embraces one week & one day—

THE 27th.—Rio Rojo—Cross Timbers.—Buffaloe wolves & buzzards.—a Rivulet.—Far west and the mormons.—The 28th.—Red River again.—Bulls.—pit in the sand.—camp.—violent Storm. . guard.—The 29th. combat entre deux.—Camp.—Cooper and Harden.—combat second.— Bonnie Black Bess.—The hunters' success.—Boucannierring 30th The tragical fate of Bonnie Bess.—heavy dews and sand-burs.—Early Start.—mules missed.—Bulls.—a road cut by the

Sappers.—a wild Turkey.—The 1st of October.—Cow Shot.—long days—camp.—2nd. No dew. Travel till noon.—Rio Rojo —an island.—2 deer.—Bands of Buffaloe.—Turkies.—The pointed Buttes.—Jeffers & Harden kill a Cow.—Linn & Dewey Kill 2 Bulls.—Janvier and François kill 2 also within 300 yards of camp.—Rouchon. Belanger & Revon kill 5 cows.—The 3rd— River crossed—coolness of the atmosphere.—herds of Bison. Fitzpatrick wounds a cow.—camp in a bottom—rain.—The 4th. —Stay in camp till 12. deer killed by Bowers.—cold & rain.— no human signs.—travel to a creek 3 miles distant & camp.

The morning of the 27th broke fair and sunny, and at an early hour our caballada descended into the bed of the Canadian and crossed to its northern shore. The water was, in this place barely flowing.—Its depth was about 6 inches and of the channel which was fully a mile in breadth, it occupied about one 50th part.

T'is a peculiarity of the Canadian as well as of most of these mountain streams which flow across the level prairie, in their passage to the ocean, that for several hundred miles from their source or springs, their bed is generally well supplied with water, which is diminished in quantity as it flows, untill it reaches those vast beds of sand, which constitute the channel of the Canadian, below the Cañons, and then is swallowed up by these thirsty resorvoirs, or is so exhausted by the draws upon its volume as to be scarcely able to flow afterwards. Again it happens perhaps that the explorer after pursuing the parched up channel for several leagues without beholding so much water as would quench his burning thirst, again reaches a sudden spring or out gushing of the confined element from the sands, and follows for miles afterwards a rolling river, again to be lost and again to burst its bonds, and gush forth to pursue its destined journey towards the Father of Waters or the Gulfe of Mexico. The cognomen applied by the Spanish travellers to a river of this description which flows through Texas, or rather whose channel lies in Texas, was well chosen & is most expressive of [the] thing as it really is. El Rio Perdido might just as well be applied to the Canadian as it presents itself to the eye at this point.

We passed over to the opposite side without difficulty and launched into the forest of black-jack[1] and post oak which now covered the country in connected patches for miles ahead.

"The Celebrated Cross Timbers["] (observes Gregg in his commerce of the prairies.) ["]of which frequent mention has been made, extend from the Brazos, or perhaps from the Colorado of Texas, across the sources of Trinity, traversing Red River above the false Wachita and thence W of N to the Red fork of Arkansas, if not farther."[2]

Passing the spot, wherat the hunters had left the slain buffaloe the preceding evening, we beheld a great quantity of buzzards hovering over and alighting upon the almost fleshless remains. A wolf also was noticed to sneak away among the forest trees and hollows.

After crossing a number of deep worn hollows, in which were running rivulets of clear water, we halted about 12 o'clock, on the banks of one of them, and camped for the day.

Some shouldered their rifles and sallied forth among the hills & woods, which extended on every side, to search for deer and turkies. Others took the occasion to enjoy a nap—some to wash their garments in the pure water of the creek and others again took their needles and employed themselves in manufacturing fancy-fringed pants of the dressed buffaloe cow skins procured from among the Kiowas above. There was yet another class besides all these, otherwise engaged. There were several in our com-

---

[1] The blackjack is an oak that grows thirty to fifty feet high. Its short, spreading branches form a narrow, round-topped, often irregular head. Its range is from New York to Florida, and westward to Texas and Nebraska. Bailey, *Cyclopedia of American Horticulture*, III, 1479.

[2] The quotation is on page 360 in the edition edited by Max L. Moorhead.

pany who had served in the famous campaign, against the latter-day Saints, yclept the Mormon War. Hardy old veterans were they and many a wonderful yarn was spun by them for our edification concerning the sacking of that stronghold of Smithism & Mormonism.—Far West, and the expulsion of the whole sect from Missouri.[3]

The 28th saw us again recross the Canadian and wend our way along its southern side, across hollows and gaps which might be comparatively denominated embryo cañons. Towards evening however we found ourselves performing what might be called a short cut, across a bend of the river which encircled a prairie almost level. Our pilot conducted us into a dense bottom between the Canadian and the hills and having reached a clear place near the river, about camping hour, we pitched our tents, and drove our animals to the opposite side of the river's bed.

We judged from the appearance of 4 or 5 buffaloe bulls[4] in that direction, that there was water there, and our conjectures were not unfounded. A pit was also dug by us in the sand, near our encampment and good water procured both for drinking and culinary purposes.

Thus far I had allotted for my riding a black mare, which had been once a wild mustang. A beautiful head, with long, silken jet black main and flowing tail, gave her a most beautiful look, but her strength was insufficient to carry her through the fearful ordeal, by which so many animals yearly perish. Her back had been injured by the chafing of the saddle and during the few past

[3] "Mormon War," obviously not the 1857–58 expedition to Utah led by Colonel Albert Sidney Johnston, refers to much earlier troubles in Missouri. Mormons settled at Independence in 1833 but were driven out by mob action. They fared little better in Clay County, and in 1838 they established the county seat of Far West in newly formed Calhoun County. Violence continued, and in 1838 Governor Lilburn Boggs of Missouri called out the militia to oust the Mormons from Missouri. They then settled in Nauvoo, Illinois. Edwin C. McReynolds, *Missouri: A History of the Crossroads State,* 137–44.

[4] Buffalo seen now were all bulls. Abert, *Guádal P'a,* 92, says, "The sexes are said generally to separate at this season."

days she had been running loose, the flies so bad in this immediate region fastened upon her and ruined her forever.

Tonight she sank down, unable to go farther. The wind became very violent towards 9 o'clock and continued to increase in strength for some time. Heavy black clouds gathered over our horizon like a pall, and at 10, the heavy rain, accompanied by lurid lightning and deafning thunder, drove before the wind, and descended upon us with the weight of hail. I was on duty as night guard during the entire storm and I shall never forget the fearful scene.—Drenched with cold rain from head to foot, I stood in water 3 or 4 inches deep and as cold as ice,—nothing but wet buffaloe skin moccasins upon my feet—My rifle in my hand but entirely useless.—The wind almost lifting me from my feet.—The country dangerous from prowling indians.—The night as dark as Erebus.—The lightning now and then exposing at a second, an entire camp and caballada of picketed mules—their backs to the pelting storm. Truly it was no amusement. However there was some consolation in knowing that 11½ o'clock was not far distant, and then, O how I would sleep under that waterproof tent.

"You had better awaken your mess, Cooper" said our pilot to me,[5] as he came around in the darkness during a short interval of the violent hurricane. ["]In order that they may be ready for a start in case the water rises any higher." We were encamped in a little bottom and were exposed to the full power of every drop that fell on the camp. The ground was as flat as a table and not a drop ran from it in any direction. I awoke the 2nd guard of the night, and as I groped my way into my own tent, I heard a muttered exclamation of damnd fine scrape, escape his lips, and I felt ten dollars more happy than he, untill I splashed my hands into a puddle of 6 inches deep, collected within the very tent. The men were snoozing all around me and though every blanket and robe and man in it, were reposing in mud & water still the sleepers

[5] Here François des Montaignes slips and calls himself Cooper.

slept and slept sound at that. I rolled myself up in my blankets, drew my feet up from being exposed to the rain through the entrance, laid down in the water and deposited my head in my saddle. In less than ten minutes I was sound asleep and ignorant of earthly affairs.

The morning with its bright warm sun, was greeted by us, as a dear friend, and so cheerful were his rays this day, that we almost felt tempted, to pardon his fiery acts toward us, whilst travelling over the plains.

Our blankets, robes clothing etc, together with La Tulippe's petit sac de sucre were laid out in the sun to dry. My unfortunate mare who sported the magnificent title of Bonnie Black Bess, was so invigorated by the pelting of the night's storm and so renovated by the morning's sun, as to be able to stand upon her feet and recommence her day's travel. Following the southern side of the channel for a few miles, we reached a point whence we could ascend to the main prairie. Striking from the river we travelled over the rolling prairie till noon, when we encamped at a small rivulet of cool and limpid water which afforded us a princely luxury in return for our thirsty wanderings. Three or four groups of Buffaloe were grazing within a few miles of our camp, and we had no sooner halted than, Harden and Stephen Cooper were despatched in the hunt.

They went out on foot as our meagre and badly conditioned caballada, contained no animals stout or suitable enough for the chase. Nothing but a number of lean & scarified mules and 3 or 4 exhausted ponies. The 2 still-hunters returned before dark with the meat of a cow.

At this camp, a pantomime or phantasmagora of civil war within our little troupe, was represented on the prairie, in the form of a combat entre deux.

The national peculiarities of the Canadians and Americans, naturally afforded each a subject of debate and wrangling, and had during the course of the day's travel occasioned a battle between a couple of bloods. One was of course conqueror, whilst he who turned out 2nd best, avowed his intention to have a second trial of science when we had halted. The challenge was of course accepted, & whilst the 2 hunters aforesaid went in pursuit of buffaloe, the balance of the camp assembled on the green to behold the engagement pugilistique between Monsieur Miraut and Loren Jeffers. Miraut was again knocked into pie and forced to acknowledge the crown. This evening also, was spent by some in smoking the cowskins procured from the Cayquas. A pit was dug about 18 inches in depth and about 12 in diameter, at the bottom of these a quantity of rotten wood was placed & kindled. Over this was suspended the skin, sewed in shape of a bag, and held upright by means of a couple of bent branches. The base was stretched around the edge of the hole and securely pegged so as to prevent the escape of the least smoke.

We left this fine little camping place about 7 o'clock, but Bonnie Bess was unable to accompany us, and remained on the prairie to feed the jackalls and vultures.[6] The dew was uncommonly heavy last night and so it was, at every low camping place, within the Cross Timbers.

As we journied along, 4 large bulls came lumbering towards us, no doubt mistaking us for a band of their fellows. They soon discovered their mistake however and turning at right angles, were soon lost among the groves. Our route was of course tortuous, and notwithstanding our endeavours to take advantage of the cleared spots, we were frequently compelled to halt, and cut a passage through some dense grove, or make a passway across some deep bedded creek. These groves were the abodes of innu-

[6] Bonnie Black Bess was the horse of Dick Turpin's famous ride, which Montaignes probably knew through Harrison Ainsworth's novel *Rookwood* (1834). Abert takes note of the passing of Isaac Cooper's Bonnie Black Bess in his official report. On September 30, he writes, "We were obliged to leave one of our horses here, as his back had become incurable, and was now so very sore (the blow-flies having got in) that we could not use it." *Report*, 94.

merable turkies, and though we travelled exceedingly fast when once through a strip of timber, our Sharp Shooters[7] frequently contrived to bring down a fat hen as a rarity at supper.

The first of October was likewise spent in travelling through the same aspect of country—rolling region,—dense strips and spots of timber, dotting the land over like a chess board,—clear little prairies of rich land constituting about an equal space. This will in the course of time, become the abode of civilized agriculture. The clear spots will become fields of plenty—The groves will echo to the woodman's axe and the deerhunters gun.—Yon aspiring mound will be the seat, either of a town or villa,—whilst the clear voice of the merry farmer, the prattle of flaxan headed children,—the bleat of sheep-flocks,—the neigh of horses and the sound of herds, will break the silence which now broods over this neutral ground of Barbarism and Demi Civilization. The Camanche and Cayqua—The Pawnee & the Osage will then no longer roam through its solitude and over its rich grounds, unconscious of the advantages he spurns, and seeking only for murder and barbarian revenge.

The region of the Cross Timbers is, in fact the most beautiful and the most suitable for agriculture, of any tract between the settlements and the mountains.

We saw many buffaloe during the course of the day, many of which were running towards the south as if pursued by Indian hunters. A cow was brought down by Solomon Rivar, and the meat brought into camp.

The days were long, and we generally made a good days travel, considering the obstacles to be overcome.

Our camp was on a little rivulet of beautiful water, whose banks were covered with dense growths of greenbriar and willow. Some huge cottonwoods likewise added a feature to the picture.

---

[7] An early, but not the earliest, use of the term Sharp Shooters, which some have mistakenly derived from the Sharps rifle of the Civil War period.

There was no dew to night and the wind blew till morning. Feeling very much refreshed by the fresh buffaloe meat and the fresh water, we pushed on till 12 o'clock and camped again on the north bank of the River. Our camp was pitched near the edge of the bed, which was a couple of hundred feet below us. There was a couple of feet of water in the channel & was flowing gently. A large island stood in the channel, and during the course of the day we saw several deer come down to drink.

Over the country on the opposite side of the river, were scattered numerous bands of buffaloe, whilst on our side, 3 or 4 bands could be seen within the distance of 3 or 4 miles.

The men as usually sallied out to hunt, and Jeffers and Harden brought down a cow.—Linn & Dewey killed a couple of bulls.—Belanger—Rouchon—and Rivar killed 5 cows and brought in a quantity of meat. Janvier and François des Montaignes being unsuccessful in the hunt, having seen but a couple of wild turkies, returned to camp, but, perceiving a couple of veteran bulls seeking water in the channel above, they again seized their guns and sallied up the bank. Advancing about a mile above the camp, the[y] suddenly came upon the 2 bulls, who had just emerged from the channel to the prairie. They levelled their guns and fired. One ran a few yards and fell dead,—shot through the heart. The other stopped to look for his comrade and received a second discharge & fell. They were both very large and the first measured 12 feet from the tip of the snout to the tail—18 inches between the butts of the horns and ten feet around the belly. Towards dusk the air turned quite cool, and the wind blew violently, and during my guard (middle watch), the rain fell in large drops. This was our first introduction to cool weather.

In the morning (the 3rd) we descended the steep bank with our mules and waggons and travelled down in the bed for a mile. Reaching a bottom on the left hand, we followed it during 3 hours. Many buffaloe were on every side, and as a gang of about 150 or 200 rushed along ahead of our caballada Mr. Fitzpatrick wounded a cow, but she did not fall.

We camped in a dense bottom which looked so wild & desolate, as to forbid all idea of man ever having been there. It commenced to rain towards evening and continued at intervals till morning (4th). We remain here encamped, whilst Mr. Fitzpatrick rode out to examine the route. He returned about 12 and we left the camp and the River. A deer very fat was killed & brought into camp last night by Bowers.[8] T'was likewise tolerably cool.

Our veteran La Tulippe confessed having once been in these parts, but selon Jamieson who is pretty much of a wag, The old man would say he had been in the moon, if he knew that thar war any Bièvres or Blackfeet there.

CHAPTER SEVENTEEN

In which 2 Remarkble personages
of Nicholas Nickelby and Humphrey Clock memory
are introduced
in
New Circumstances.
viz Fanny Squears & Sally Brass

THE 5th Oct.—Buffaloe.—rain. The 6th.—Rain. cold. The 7th.—Small creek flowing south.— day guard.—pursuit of 3 Buffaloes by François des Montaignes.

[8] Abert, *Report*, 96, notes the hugeness of this deer: "When we first noticed it lying on the ground, deprived of its skin, it was mistaken by some for one of our small oxen. Its extraordinary size and fatness made us only regret that our friends towards the east could not share in our enjoyments."

The 8th.—small creek.—Fanny Squears in a quandary. Buffaloe again.—hanks appear.—The 9th.—good equestrianism.—last band of buffaloe.—Indians supposed to be seen.—deer.—the River.—camp—good water.—stumps of felled trees—The 10th. —2nd day's walk.—Bête-puant or polecat.—first swine seen. —persimmons.—Rivan kills 2 Turkies.—The fort or trading post of Chouteau—a trail.—Crows.—Camp in a clump of briars.— scarce water.—The 11th.—Fanny Squears restored to health and to the saddle.—early Start.—tangled route.—road making.— travel thus 5 miles. Camp.—persimmons.—trees blazed and pictured.—the skull of a buffaloe fixed on a pole.—a deer head ditto. —start at 12 o'clock.—travel till 4.—Camp on the side of a hill. —scarce water.—Sally Brass having given out and remained behind during the course of the day, rejoins the Caballada during the night.—a possum.—The 12th.—Start before Sunrise—travel 7 miles and halt at a spring.—firing in the woods.—dreadful fate of 2 hogs.—fresh mule tracts seen in the woods.—more blazed trees.— old Indian camps.—smoke ahead and Indians. The 13th. —travel 17 miles still on the trail.—Red River one mile distant. —Indian cows and horses.—camp in a bottom by a creek.— squirrels and grapes.—The 14th.—a Kickapoo Village.—houses, fences, fields and cattle.—ducks, geese,—flying squirrel, hanks, haws, grapes, Bois-d'arc—Osage apples.—A Quapa Indian.— The 15th.—ascend the hills & pursue a North East Course.— thick woods,—groves of hickory.—axes heard.—a Muscogee clearing.—$\frac{1}{2}$ mile to a trading house.—Whiskey $2.00 per gallon.—no guard.—negroes and Indians.—seminoles.—duck Shooting.—a Grand Spree.—an Indian dance.—Tobacco.— lead.—powder traded off for Corn.—an American & his Squaw. (Old Edwards.)
The 16th. Cross the Creek.—Report of the annexation of Texas. —another report.—devastations of a hurricane—the road.—old fort.—farms. several Indians on foot.—Report concerning the

invasion of the panis & Mahas.—we feed our animals,—pass a
stony hill.—a Blacksmith Shop.—an Irish vulcan married to a
Cherokee Venus.—Our camp. hog killed.—our Spanish heifer
bartered for corn and the last killed for meat.

The creek we camped on the night of the 4th, was 3 miles from
our camp in the river bottom.

Leaving this the following morning, we travelled industriously
all day. There were plenty of buffaloe over the prairie and a bull
was killed.—We camped on a creek and spent this night and the
following day (6th). We also travelled a long day's journey on
the 7th and encamped on a little creek, flowing towards the south,
& emptying into the Canadian which was in sight.[1]

Being day guard for the evening, I saw 3 buffaloe bulls in the
prairie, & following them for 2 miles.

On the 8th, we camped on another little rivulet, whilst a band
of buffaloe grazed undisturbed on the adjacent swells.

Miss Fanny Squears,[2] who, be it know[n], was no other than a
diminutive black mule with long ears & short legs, in attempting
to reach a certain little puddle of water, in the rivulet bed, became suddenly and most unexpectedly bemired, and would most
certainly have remained there untill death, if the guard had not
raised the alarm, and the anxious camp flew to her rescue.

A multitude of hawks flew around our camp at dusk, and our
Captain amused himself in discharging his shotgun ineffectually
at them as they playfully wheeled around him.

[1] This camp was about two miles south of present-day Mustang, Oklahoma, near
Oklahoma City, on a small stream flowing into the Canadian one and one-half miles
away. Abert, *Guádal P'a*, 98, note 278.

[2] Miss Fanny Squeers (not Squears), a character in *Nicholas Nickleby*, was
daughter of the master of Dotheboys Hall, and, says Charles Dickens, "If there be
any one grace or loveliness inseparable from that particular period of life (23 years),
Miss Squeers may be presumed to have been possessed of it, as there is no reason to
suppose that she was a solitary exception to a universal rule." From her mother "she
inherited a voice of harsh quality," and from her father "a remarkable expression of
the right eye, something akin to having none at all."

The morning was that of the 9th, and shouldering my rifle, I tripped it á pied, over the prairie in advance of the company.—A band of buffaloe hove in sight, I crawled within 100 yards of them, but the inopportune appearance of our caballada on a hill alarmed them & my shot proved ineffectual. We travelled about 23 miles along a dividing ridge between the waters of North & South Fork.

Several hunters of our party as they extended their researches to a couple of miles on each side reported having seen Indians, but these not appearing afterwards inclined us to disbelieve their reports.[3]

Approaching the river, we encamped on a clear rivulet of cold water flowing into it, frightening, as we halted, 2 splendid deer which had been concealed in the clumps of sumach. I was much fatigued of course with my efforts & still more so, on account of my worn out and hard moccasins, which lacerated and blistered my feet, as I trod over the dead grass which had now changed from the buffaloe grass into the long dead grass of the border.

I continued my pilgrimage on the 10th and walked 21 or 22 miles.—A bête puant or pole cat crossed my path and I killed it, the smell proceeding from it, reached a comrade 1½ miles below me.—Some hogs were noticed by Ralph the black cook, who supposed they were wild.—persimmon trees appeared today.

Solomon who walked with me today killed 2 wild turkies.—on crossing a small creek several yards in width, and bordered on each side by a strip of tangled bottom, briars, trees and vines 50 yards in breadth, we came suddenly upon the site where once stood the old trading fort of Monsieur Chouteau. "Just at hand["] says Gregg, ["]there was a beautiful spring, where in 1835,

[3] Says Abert, *Guádal P'a*, 99, "We despatched two of our men to get meat . . . they returned saying that they had seen two Indians. . . . We expected all day that these Indians would visit us, but were disappointed and should have concluded that our men were mistaken, had we not known them both to be experienced in prairie life."

157

Col. Mason with a force of U.S. Troops had a 'big talk,' and a still 'bigger smoke' with a party of Comanche and Witchita Indians. ["] [4]

This fort was erected by Col. Chouteau in 1836 and abandoned in the commencement of 1839.—This trader died at Fort Gibson at the same time. All that now remained of the Fort, were 3 or 4 upright posts and 2 rough stone chimnies blackened by time. [5]

Revan who had lived here when a boy, and myself mounted these monuments of past greatness and waved our handkerchiefs over their ruins. [6] A road wound down from the fort and conducted us through some difficult points of the Cross Timbers. This trail winds off towards the Arkansas and has been made doubtlessly by the traders and is perhaps the same one travelled by Josiah Gregg in 1839.—We pursued the trail till near dusk, when we encamped in a bottom of dense and matted greenbriar.—Crows were plenteous for the first time. The raven is the crow of the prairies.—water was likewise scarce.

The morrow of the 11th was fine and Fanny Squears having recovered from her indisposition was again restored to the saddle, and performed her duty faithfully during the day.—The woods were extremely tangled and we travelled but 5 miles, when we

[4] Auguste Pierre Chouteau (1787–1838), eldest son of Pierre Chouteau, Sr., attended West Point but resigned his commission in 1807 to take charge of the Arkansas branch of the fur trade. He established a trading post on the site of Camp Holmes, also called Camp Mason, near present Lexington, McClain County, Oklahoma, not to be confused with Fort Holmes in Hughes County. Richard Barnes Mason was major in 1835, becoming lieutenant colonel in 1836 and colonel in 1846. In the treaty the Comanches and Wichitas agreed to maintain friendly relations with Cherokees, Creeks, Choctaws, Osages, Senecas, and Quapaws, recently moved to Indian Territory. Gregg, *Commerce*, 231 and notes.

[5] Abert: ". . . we entered the tangled bottom of Chouteau's Creek. Soon after crossing it, we were cheered by the sight of the ruins of Old Fort Holmes, A lofty gate-post was leaning mournfully over the ruins around, borne down by the weight of declining years and the ravages of time. Here we saw fragments of wagons, which, by their age, showed that the place had long been deserted." *Guádal P'a*, 99–100.

[6] Abert: "Some of our people, in the height of their enthusiasm, mounted the chimney, and unfurled the American handkerchief, that it might float in the breeze. It was a grateful sight to all once more to meet certain vestiges of the white men." *Ibid.*, 100.

reached a little stream. Here we halted to rest. Persimmon trees grew along this creek, whilst along the road we saw many trees blazed with some sharp instrument, and figures of Indians and animals pictured therein with gunpowder. A skull of a buffaloe,— that of a deer etc, were noticed stuck upon poles along the road. We left this halting place at 12 o'clock and travel[ed] along the trail till 4. We camped on the side of a hill and though there was no water for the mules and barely anough for the men, we remained there this night and started at daybreak. Miss Sally Brass,[7] another famous quadruped of our caballada having given out during the day, rejoined her comrades during the night but was again abandoned the following day. We never saw her again. A small possem perfectly white was shot at this camp.

Travelling 7 miles we stopped at a fine spring which gushed from the side of a hill, and remained at this place for 3 hours.— During this time however, a band of hogs, tame ones without doubt & belonging to the Indian settlements approached our camp. Our men being unused to such sights and ignorant of our near approach to civilization levelled their rifles and shot at a brace of these too unsuspicious quadrupeds, and more would doubtless have been killed, had not some one discovered that their ears were marked.

The deceased swine were quickly despoiled of their hide and hair, and afforded a luxurious banquet to our hungry band.[8]

A gun was also heard in the woods but there being at the moment no one of our party absent, t'was conjectured that some civilized Indian was about.

[7] Miss Sally Brass was another character created by Dickens in *The Old Curiosity Shop*, published with *Barnaby Rudge* in 1841 under the general title *Master Humphrey's Clock*, which is mentioned in the summary chapter heading. "Miss Sally Brass, then, was a lady of thirty-five, or thereabouts, of a gaunt and bony figure and a resolute bearing, which, if it suppressed the softer emotions of love, and kept admirers at a distance, certainly inspired a feeling akin to awe in the breasts of those male strangers who had the happiness to approach her."

[8] A few days later it was learned that these hogs had been running wild for years and were fair game for all. Abert, *Guádal P'a*, 105–106.

Fresh mule tracks were likewise noticed in the forest. Travelling on till evening, and passing several old camping grounds of Indian bands, we beheld towards the East about sunset, a group of figures, which we supposed were mounted Indians, but as they quickly disappeared, we were in doubt. A thick smoke likewise rose up from the northern horizon.

We camped on a rocky little rivulet, and the appearance of a score of fine fat cows red and black, which approached our camp, confirmed us in our opinion of the proximity of civilized tribes.

Making an early start on the morning of the 13th, we still pursued the trail,—and having cast our eyes upon the last cactus covered as it was with a quantity of mellow fruit, we once more approached the Canadian and camped on a little rivulet, about one mile distant from it. Distance of today 17 miles.

Hickory was a principal tree seen today. Starting before daybreak on the 14th, we reached within a mile, a large Kickapoo village, containing about 300 buildings, with fields, fences etc. Yet not a single living person could we see. They were out perhaps, on a buffaloe hunt on the prairie. These were their cows and horses. But they themselves were perhaps many miles from us.

The river was here flowing in several places: wild-ducks and a number of geese were sporting in its waters, whilst in the woods, chattered squirrels and hawks. The forest was filled with grapes & haws. Large trees covered the river bottom and vines strewed the ground. A couple having gone out to hunt down the river returned at evening with a Quapaw Indian on horseback. He was one of a nation which formerly resided North of Fort Gibson, but which is now very much scattered & diminished. He had a fine looking steed, he was about 6 feet several inches in heigth himself, & with his scarf around his head and his leather hunting shirt, presented a most picturesque appearance. He gave us some instructions concerning the route across the hills, and then left us.[9] On the 15th, therefore we again left the Canadian,

and mounting the hills, journied in a North Eastern direction,—
the woods were very dense, frequently interspersed with clumps
of hickory sometimes of tolerable size. Many little hollows or ravines had to be crossed, and their banks were invariably guarded
by an impenetrable hedge of briars and brush. The welcome sound
of an axe, greeted our ears, from the forest, about 3 o'clock, and
our eyes were feasted with the sight of an Indian log-raising. A
number, of Creek or Muscoghee Indians,[10] were building a log-
house.—"½ a mile to a trading house" said they. We rode into
a kind of village or hamlet of Indian houses and fields, a store,
etc. The first enquiry of some of our party was for fire water. Fire
water was $2 a gallon. The boys had no money.—The boys had
handkerchiefs and shirts. Ergo: the handkerchiefs & shirts were
given for whiskey and the boys became literally high. Shirt after
shirt was bartered for quart after quart and boy after boy became
drunk. Some stood up and some lay down, some yelled and
some remained silent some talked and some sang and some became funny and talked, some considered themselves perfectly
majestic and powerful & 3 or 4 picked up others and would have
thrown them into the fire out of joke. Towards night there were
not 5 sober men in the camp.—An Indian dance not far distant
lent its assistance to the scene. The mules were in a stock field,
no guard was necessary, and about midnight the hogs of the

[9] Abert: "In the afternoon Yount brought in a fine and intelligent looking Indian,
who belonged to a small tribe called 'Quapaws'. . . . He told us that some of his
people were encamped a few miles below us and the rest, with the Kickapoos . . .
had gone off to their hunting grounds. We asked him how far we should have to go
before meeting with white people. He replied that we could start in the morning
and reach them before the sun attained its mid-day height." *Ibid.*, 103–104. The
Quapaws, or Arkansas, were a Siouan people, among the first to be allotted land in
Indian Territory. They were situated in the northeastern corner, where many Eastern
tribes joined them. The Kickapoos were an Algonquian people of Wisconsin and
Illinois.

[10] Abert says the Creeks "were most tastefully dressed in handsome shawls grace-
fully twisted around their heads. They also wore leggins and moccasins of buckskin,
handsome calico shirts, and beautiful pouches, with broad belts ornamented with
massive bead work." *Ibid.*, 105.

161

neighbourhood were running away with the meat, the bread, the kettles and the mule collars.

This was the night of the 15th. Even men who had never perhaps drank a gill in their life, were tempted that evening to drink untill they became stupid.

At this place we saw an old Tenessean married to an Indian squaw. He was doing fine and had grown daughters.

At the store at this place, also, our powder lead and tobacco were bartered away for corn, as we were now entering a country where grazing was precarious and vegetation at the same time entirely dry & withered.

We left this place in the morning of the 16th, crossed the creek and travelled over a sandy road through a well wooded & well watered country. A few farms appeared along the road. as also a large wooden fort or block house in ruins. We likewise met a waggon coming from Van Buren—as also 2 Indians on foot bringing dressed deer skins. At the place we had left we first heard of the annexation of Texas to the United States, with the further report of a great battle between the United States troops and the Mexicans, in which 700 Americans had entirely defeated 1700 Mexicans.

This last report though very false was perfectly accredited by us, who were ready to believe anything. We were informed also that during the last winter the country had been infested by the Pawnee & Mahas, who had committed great depredations.

About 3 miles from the settlement, we passed a portion of country, wheron all the forest trees great and small were bent to the earth, some broken off close to the ground, others splintered and some torn up by the roots. The tract of the whirlwind or tornado was about $\frac{1}{2}$ mile broad and appeared to come from the North East. We stopped at noon to feed our animals and again proceeded on our route. After crossing a stony range of hills we reached about dusk a blacksmith shop, an Irishman married to an Indian woman. From him we procured some pork. Our last beeves were here disposed of. One was killed for beef and the other exchanged for corn wherewith to feed our famished animals.

CHAPTER EIGHTEEN

THE 17th.—travellers of the Indian country.—Cherokee region.—18th.—Agent of the Seminoles—an Indian farm.—a field of Cotton.—The North Fork.—Negro farm.—sweet potatoes.—The 19th.—purchase Corn.—Texian emigrants.—old stockfield.—a traveller from Fort Gibson.—his report.—The 20th.—North Course.—21st.—a Seminole hamlet.—poor Indians.—Belanger's arrival,—an officer from Fort Ouachita,—The Arkansas bottom,—a drunken Indian. —More Texian emigrants.—their report.—The 22nd.—The ferry and ferryman of the Arkansas.—sandboats.—Indian killing ducks. The canebrakes.—The fording of the Arkansas and that of the Neosho.—Walloon Shooting.—Our entrance into Fort Gibson. 23rd.—24th—25—26th.—27th—28th—29th & 30th.

Pursuing the now beaten road which led to Fort Gibson, we met a negro and negress,[1]—3 Americans etc,[2] and camped at evening within a mile of a farm & 4 from a Cherokee village.

Indian ponies were gambolling around us and the country

[1] Abert comments: "We met several Negroes on the road who were dressed in the picturesque costume of the Creek Indians, which certainly becomes them well. They are said to acquire the different languages with great facility." *Guádal P'a*, 108.

[2] Abert: "The most astonishing sight which had greeted our eyes for a long while was three white men, who were dressed in scarlet leggins, with immense scarlet scarfs about their necks. They were certainly laboring under some strange hallucination. We rejoiced to see them free in this wild country, where there were no lunatic asylums." *Ibid.*

presented all the appearances of our most familiar landscapes.

On the 18th,—we met the agent of the Seminole nation, with 2 carriages, on his way to pay them their annuity,[3]—he reported having lost a couple of horses a few days back, whether stolen or strayed he knew not. We halted to noon near an Indian farm, and towards evening reached the North Fork. A number of houses and fields, apparently belonging to Negroes, were congregated at this point, & this night we encamped in a cottonfield. The North Fork at this point is a clear but swift stream and flows between 2 high banks, part of its bed is rock and in some places is deep. It is easily forded and we crossed it in a quarter of an hour. Sweet potatoes were procured by the boys in return for rice, and afforded a great luxury to the hungry.

The following morning, before starting we took in a suitable supply of shelled corn, & pursued our route, passing several waggons of Emigrants bound to Texas. We camped on a small creek, and having rented a stockfield from an Indian placed our mules in it.

A traveller passed at dusk on his way from Fort Gibson and reported it 30 miles distant. He informed us that the Comanches were then in council on the Brazos with the Texians.—That General Taylor was at Corpus Christi, and that we would come to good water, wood & grass within 10 miles.

In the morning therefore our caravan started before daybreak, and following the road which led in a Northern direction, though a raw wind, we reached the camping ground mentioned. Black haws were in great abundance on all the streams of this country: a traveller & his spouse remained in our camp to night.

We remained encamped at this place till 12 o'clock the following day (the 21st) in expectation of the arrival of Messrs. Abert

[3] Abert: "Early this morning we passed a couple of wagons, accompanied by three or four men, and afterwards learned that they contained large amounts of specie, which the Indian agent who accompanied them was conveying across the country to make his payments." *Ibid.*, 109.

& Peck who had left us at the crossing of the North fork, to explore its course to its mouth. They not arriving at the abovementioned hour, we saddled up and pursued our route.—Belanger who had accompanied the 2 gentlemen above mentioned, soon overtook us, as also, an officer and attendants on their way from Fort Ouachita on Red River to Fort Gibson on the Neosho or Grand.[4] We camp within a mile of the Arkansas, and expect to enter Fort Gibson tomorrow. To spend the interval however, a drunken Indian stalks into our camp and accuses us of stealing and butchering one of his cows. He had been wise to have kept silent, for had he not been drunk the unfortunate devil would have found himself in no weak hands. As it was our grey haired leader repented of not having kicked him out of camp.

A large number of emigrants from Jackson Missouri, to Texas on the Trinity camped near us, and the sight of their waggons, their sheep, horses, hogs, dogs, children & merry girls, recalled the scenes to be witnessed at home. They reported the last season to have been quite unhealthy in the West, and we had proof of the assertion in the place we were, for all around us, white and Indian, from North Fork to Springfield Mo, were bleached with sickness and disease.

The 22nd.—Today we descended into the rich alluvial bottom of the Arkansas and in about ¾ of an hour attained the crossing.

Fort Gibson reared its white walls and chimnies about 2 miles distant on the East bank of the Neosho which here debouches into the Arkansas. A gigantic Negro, whose language was so mixed up with Indian as to be almost unintelligible to us, presented himself as ferryman and demanded a dollar per waggon for ferriage.

4 Abert and Peck were trying to fix the point of junction of the South Fork of the Canadian with the Arkansas. After studying the situation, they sent Belanger (who had accompanied them) back to the expedition with word that they intended to remain where they were until they could obtain a satisfactory series of observations. Fitzpatrick was to lead the expedition rapidly on to Fort Gibson and there await the arrival of the lieutenants. *Ibid.*, 109–10.

The waggons were loaded into the flat boat by hand, whilst the loose mules etc, and the mounted men, forded the River above the entrance of the Neosho, and then easily forded the latter. A number of boats laden with sand were steaming the current towards the Fort, and 3 or 4 stout Indians laden with ducks were wading among the gravel beds. Along the bank on the East stretched impenetrable jungles of perpendicular canes emphatically called cane brakes.—a Walloon[5] was dipping & diving in the River, whilst our Sharp Shooters attempted in vain to pierce him with a ball as he rose to the surface.

Our dirty but ruddy looking band[6] filed into the little town which sports the name of Fort, whilst the lean, lank legged, leather sided regulars gazed at our plump figures, the plumper by comparison with our jaded mules, with an envious eye, and as we arrived the commanding officer sent in a request, very modest to be sure, that some of us would gratify him by enlisting. Poor fellows, we would do [no] such a thing and Fort Gibson didn't get a single man. We were pretty short of provisions, and the rations he sent us were received in a more cordial manner than the request. The bread, the flour,—the mess pork,—the beans,— the sugar & the coffee suffered under our attack, whilst our little camp was always crowded with sargeants, drum majors, and soldiers of every description, who sat around our fires & listened half the night to the interminable yarns invented by our most waggish Sindbads. The Indians we had seen & fought the men we had lost, the spanish towns we had triumphantly taken in our route and the wonders we had seen, were themes never to be sufficiently expatiated upon, only to be admired.

One of our wags, a fellow weighing about 200, & as round and

[5] Presumably he means a loon.

[6] Abert: ". . . we were dressed in buckskin trousers, with fringed seams; shirts of bright red flannel, and calico of all colors; our hair long and wild; our faces sunburnt and unshaven; and, with our rifles flung across the saddlebow, we presented a formidable, not to say ferocious appearance." *Journal*, 105.

as ruddy as a golden pippin, had the audacity to tell his war like audience, that we had lately very lately, narrowly escaped being starved to death.

Several of the mules were here shod & some exchanged.—One of our men, Rouchon, being offered a good salary to carry on his profession as stonecutter chose to remain.

There were a quantity of Indio-niggers congregated at this place, who were moving around the fort, and were expecting emancipation the following year. These were extremely pious, and the sound of their voices, united in religious hymn & psalm were nightly heard, from their sylvan village above the Fort. The Indians immediately in the vicinity of Fort Gibson are Cherokees, and the houses around are principally occupied by families of this nation.

On the whole we enjoyed ourselves exceedingly. The place was beautiful, but with all its beauty, and all the warlike splendour of its masters, the soul stirring beat of Ros-bif,—Reveille & Tattoo, were insuf[ficient to persuade?] us to forsake our independe[nce.]

[At this point the journal comes to an abrupt end, because the remaining pages of the original manuscript have been torn into small fragments. One half-page which is still readable is written in the upright, vertical hand, indicating that this was the beginning of Chapter Nineteen. It reads:

Creek 12 Times.—distance 15 miles.—stop at a pill-Shop— signs of the time.—meet emigrants in large numbers.
We arrived at St. Louis about the
middle of November
having been out on the prairie since the 10th of
June 1845.

Abert details the last lap of the journey:

The way from Fort Gibson was literally lined with the

wagons of emigrants to Texas, and from this time untill we arrived at St. Louis we continued daily to see hundreds of them.

On the 27th we reached Maysville, where Lieutenant Peck left us, in order to go round by the way of Westport to take charge of some baggage belonging to the party, which had been left there on setting out. Our route across the States of Arkansas and Missouri afforded but little food for comment; it was too well known to give value to observations such as a rapid journey would admit.

We passed through Maysville and Bentonville, in the State of Arkansas, and Springfield, Waynesville, and Manchester, in the State of Missouri.

On the evening of the 12th of November we arrived safely at St. Louis. The next morning the men were paid and discharged, and the public property in my care was turned over to Mr. Robert Campbell, the government agent, with directions that it be sold at public auction. Abert, *Guádal P'a,* 113.]

THE BREAKS & THE EXPEDITION

Friend or foe, 'tis all the same
Read here the travels of Montaignes.
Though F. des M. be not his name,
This is, sans doute, from his own brain,
    And is most true, I tell you all,
    As sure as Adam had a fall.

The trip was one of those mad freaks
Which a fool alone forever seeks
'T was one brimfull of venture wild,
Of tempests strong and sunshine mild

And is most true, I tell you all,
As sure as Adam had a fall.

The writer is not mad, I spose,
Though he may seem so to his foes
And these same pages, illy brook,
By any one, so to look.
    They are most true I tell you all
    As sure as Adam had a fall.

For their descriptions nought is asked
But that in favour they may bask
And not like goods which lie about
On shelves as if unable to go out
    For it is most true, I tell you all
    As sure as Adam had a fall.

◆

BIBLIOGRAPHY

Abert, James William. *Guádal P'a.* Ed. and annotated by H. Bailey Carroll. Canyon, Texas, 1941.

——. *Journal of Lieutenant J. W. Abert from Bent's Fort to St. Louis in 1845.* Washington, 1846.

Adams, Ramon F. *Western Words.* New ed., Norman, 1968.

Bailey, L. R. *Indian Slave Trade in the Southwest.* Los Angeles, 1966.

Bailey, Liberty Hyde. *Cyclopedia of American Horticulture.* 4 vols. New York, 1900–1902.

Barry, Louise, comp. "Kansas Before 1854: A Revised Annals," Parts Thirteen–Fifteen, *Kansas Historical Quarterly*, Vol. XXX, No. 1 (Spring, 1964), 62–91; No. 2 (Summer, 1964), 209–44; No. 3 (Autumn, 1964), 339–412.

Bashford, Herbert, and Harr Wagner. *A Man Unafraid.* San Francisco, 1927.

169

Brandon, William. *The Men and the Mountain, Frémont's Fourth Expedition.* New York, 1955.

Carson, Christopher. *Kit Carson's Autobiography.* Ed. by Milo Milton Quaife. Lincoln, 1966.

Chittenden, Hiram Martin. *The American Fur Trade of the Far West.* New York, 1935.

Clark, William Philo. *The Indian Sign Language.* Philadelphia, 1885.

Clarke, Dwight L. *Stephen Watts Kearny.* Norman, 1961.

Cline, Gloria Griffen. *Exploring the Great Basin.* Norman, 1963.

Cody, Iron Eyes. *How: Sign Talk in Pictures.* Hollywood, Calif., 1952.

Dorsey, George Amos. *Traditions of the Skidi Pawnee.* Boston, 1904.

Duffus, R. L. *The Santa Fe Trail.* London, New York, and Toronto, 1930.

Ellis, Edward S. *The Life and Times of Christopher Carson.* New York, 1899.

Estergreen, M. Morgan. *Kit Carson.* Norman, 1962.

Favour, Alpheus H. *Old Bill Williams, Mountain Man.* Norman, 1962.

Frémont, John Charles. *Memoirs of My Life.* New York, 1887.

———. *Narrative of the Exploring Expedition to the Rocky Mountains, Oregon and California.* Buffalo, 1849.

Garrard, Lewis Hector. *Wah-to-yah and the Taos Trail.* Ed. by Ralph P. Bieber. Glendale, 1938.

———. *Wah-to-yah and the Taos Trail.* Introduction by A. B. Guthrie, Jr. Norman, 1955.

Goetzmann, William H. *Army Exploration in the American West, 1803–1863.* New Haven and London, 1959.

Goodwin, Cardinal. *John Charles Frémont: An Explanation of His Career.* Stanford, 1930.

Gregg, Josiah. *Commerce of the Prairies.* Ed. by Max L. Moorhead. Norman, 1954.

Grinnell, George Bird. "Bent's Old Fort and Its Builders," *Collections of the Kansas State Historical Society,* Vol. XV (1919–22), 28–91.

———. *Beyond the Old Frontier.* New York, 1930.

———. *The Cheyenne Indians.* New Haven, 1924.

———. *Trails of the Pathfinders.* New York, 1911.

Hafen, LeRoy R., ed. *The Mountain Men and the Fur Trade of the Far West.* 8 vols. Glendale, 1965–71.

———, and W. J. Ghent. *Broken Hand: The Life Story of Thomas Fitzpatrick.* Denver, 1931.

————, and Ann W. Hafen, eds. *Frémont's Fourth Expedition*. Glendale, 1960.

————. *The Old Spanish Trail*. Glendale, 1953.

————, and Carl C. Rister. *Western America*. New York, 1941.

Heap, Gwinn Harris. *Central Route to the Pacific*. Ed. by LeRoy R. Hafen and Ann W. Hafen. Glendale, 1957.

Hoebel, Edward Adamson. *The Political Organization and Law-Ways of the Comanche Indians*. Menasha, Wis., 1940.

Hofsinde, Robert. *Indian Sign Language*. New York, 1956.

Hyde, George E. *Pawnee Indians*. Denver, 1951.

Inman, Colonel Henry. *The Old Santa Fe Trail*. New York, 1897; Topeka, 1916.

Kelly, Charles. *Old Greenwood*. Salt Lake City, 1936.

Kendall, George Wilkins. *Narrative of the Texan Santa Fe Expedition*. New York, 1844.

Lavender, David. *Bent's Fort*. Garden City, 1954.

Linton, Ralph. *The Sacrifice to the Morning Star by the Skidi Pawnee*. Chicago, 1922.

————. *The Thunder Ceremony of the Pawnee*. Chicago, 1922.

Magoffin, Susan Shelby. *Down the Santa Fe Trail and into Mexico*. Ed. by Stella M. Drumm. New Haven, 1926.

McReynolds, Edwin C. *Missouri: A History of the Crossroads State*. Norman, 1962.

Nevins, Allan. *Frémont, Pathmarker of the West*. New York and London, 1939.

————. *Frémont, the West's Greatest Adventurer*. New York, 1928.

Phillips, Paul Chrisler, and J. W. Smurr. *The Fur Trade*. 2 vols. Norman, 1961.

Pike, Zebulon Montgomery. *The Journals of Zebulon Montgomery Pike*. Ed. by Donald Jackson. 2 vols. Norman, 1966.

Preuss, Charles. *Exploring with Frémont*. Trans. and ed. by Erwin G. Gudde and Elisabeth K. Gudde. Norman, 1958.

Riddle, Kenyon. *Maps of the Old Santa Fe Trail*. Raton, N. Mex., 1953.

Rister, Carl Coke. *Border Captives*. Norman, 1940.

————. *Comanche Bondage*. Glendale, 1955.

Sabin, Edwin Legrand. *Kit Carson Days*. New York, 1935.

Stone, Irving. *Men to Match My Mountains*. Garden City, 1956.

Sunder, John E. *The Fur Trade on the Upper Missouri*. Norman, 1965.

Tomkins, William. *Universal Indian Sign Language*. San Diego, 1926.

Turner, Katharine C. *Red Men Calling on the Great White Father*. Norman, 1951.

Upham, Charles Wentworth. *Life, Explorations, and Public Services of John Charles Fremont*. Boston, 1856.

Vestal, Stanley. *Mountain Men*. Boston, 1937.

———. *The Old Santa Fe Trail*. Boston, 1939.

———. *Wagons Southwest*. New York, 1946.

Wagner, Henry R. *The Plains and the Rockies: A Bibliography*. San Francisco, 1921. Revised by Charles L. Camp. San Francisco, 1937. Third edition, revised. Columbus, Ohio, 1953.

Wallace, Edward S. *The Great Reconnaissance*. Boston and Toronto, 1955.

Wallace, Ernest, and E. Adamson Hoebel. *The Comanches, Lords of the South Plains*. Norman, 1952.

Wissler, Clark. *Indians of the United States*. New York, 1941.

INDEX

Abert, Lieutenant James William: xvi, xxiii, 41 n., 56 n., 63, 74, 77 n., 82, 156; official report of expedition, xviii, xxiv, 49–50 n.; eliminates nooning, 30 n.; discusses hunting from a stand, 45 n., 63 n.; Frémont's opinion of, 63 n.; comparison with Frémont, 74–75; comparisons between Abert's and Montaignes' journals, *see* notes on: 76, 78, 83, 90–92, 96–99, 102, 104–109, 112–23, 118–19, 124, 128, 133–36, 138, 142, 144, 148, 151, 154, 156–59, 161, 163–66; details last lap of journey, 167–68
Abert, Colonel John James: xii, xiii, 5 n.
Adonises: 109
Aeneid: 70 n.
Ainsworth, Harrison: 151 n.
Alexander the Great: 12 & n., 69
Alhambra, California: xxv
Alhambra, Texas: 134 n.
American Birds: *see* Wilson
American Desert: 45, 74, 75
American Fur Company: 4 & n.
Amphistratus: 70 n.
Amphtryon: 70 n.
Antelopes (Comanche tribe): 112 n.
Antoninus, Marcus Aurelius: 112 & n.
Apache Indians: xxiv, 27, 45, 73, 78, 90 n., 114
Arapaho Indians: xxiv, 45, 49, 53–54, 75, 114
Archambeaux (main hunter): 2 & n., 41 & n., 47
Arkansas Indians: *see* Quapaw Indians
Arkansas River: 31 n., 32, 37 n., 38, 57, 58, 60, 61, 64, 74, 75 n., 76, 81 n., 158, 165 n.; Big Bend of, 28; Red Fork of, 147
Arkansas, state of: 87
Arrow Creek (*also called* White Deer Creek): 134 & n., 135
Ascanius: 70 n.
Ashley, General William Henry: 25, 63 n.
Astor, John Jacob: 4 n.

Babylon: 9
Barnaby Rudge: 159 n.
Beaver: 143–44
Bear: 83, 88–89, 142
Bedouins of America: 73
Bedouins of the Desert: 26, 128
Belanger, Pierre: 138, 152, 165 & n.
Bent, Charles: 62 n.
Bent, William: 62 n.
Bent's Creek, trading post on: 113
Bent's Fort: xvi, 14 n., 31, 49 n., 50 n., 58–69, 74, 76 ff., 90 & n., 127, 134; entry of expedition into, 60, 62; location, 61; buildings and description, 61; inhabitants, 62, 67–69; history, 62 n.; division of expedition at, 63–64; visit from Cheyenne Indians, 64–66; traders and trappers, 67–69; livestock, 69
Bent's Post: *see* Bent's Fort
Benton, Senator Thomas Hart: xii, xiii
Bentonville, Arkansas: 168
Bête-puant soup: 107 & n.
Beulah: *see* Fisher's Hole
Bidwell, John: 63 n.
Big Horn River: 143
Big John Spring: 31 & n., 37, 38
Black Jack Creek: 26
Black Jack Grove: 26
Blackjack tree (*also called* post oak): 147 & n.
Black tail deer: 80 & n., 81
Blessington, Earl of: 124 n.
Blue (Big Blue River): 20 ff. & n., 23 & n.
Bluff Creek: *see* Little John
Boggs, Lilburn (governor of Missouri): 148 n.
Bois-de-vache: 50
Bonaparte, Charles Lucien: 33 ff., 38 n.
Bonnie Black Bess: 83, 150, 151 & n.
Boon Creek, Missouri Territory: 7 n.
Boone, Albert Gallatin: 7 n.
Boone, Daniel: 7 n.
Boone, Daniel Morgan: 7 n.
Boone's Fork: 7 & n., 9 ff., 20

173

Index

175

179

THE AMERICAN EXPLORATION AND TRAVEL SERIES

of which *The Plains* is Number 60, was started in 1939 by the University of Oklahoma Press. It follows rather logically the Press's program of regional exploration. Behind the story of the gradual and inevitable recession of the American frontier lie the accounts of explorers, traders, and travelers, which individually and in the aggregate present one of the most romantic and fascinating chapters in the development of the American domain. The following list is complete as of the date of publication of this volume:

19. Thomas D. Clark (ed.) *Travels in the Old South, 1527–1860*: A Bibliography. 3 vols.
20. Alexander Ross. *The Fur Hunters of the Far West*. Edited by Kenneth A. Spaulding.
21. W. Eugene Hollon and Ruth Lapham Butler (eds.). *William Bollaert's Texas*. Out of print.
22. Daniel Ellis Conner. *Joseph Reddeford Walker and the Arizona Adventure*. Edited by Donald J. Berthrong and Odessa Davenport.
23. Matthew C. Field. *Prairie and Mountain Sketches*. Collected by Clyde and Mae Reed Porter. Edited by Kate L. Gregg and John Francis McDermott.
24. Ross Cox. *The Columbia River*. Edited by Edgar I. and Jane R. Stewart.
25. Noel Loomis. *The Texan–Santa Fe Pioneers*.
26. Charles Preuss. *Exploring with Frémont*. Translated and edited by Edwin G. and Elisabeth K. Gudde. Out of print.
27. Jacob H. Schiel. *Journey Through the Rocky Mountains and the Humboldt Mountains to the Pacific Ocean*. Translated and edited by Thomas N. Bonner.
28. Zenas Leonard. *Adventures of Zenas Leonard, Fur Trader*. Edited by John C. Ewers.
29. Matthew C. Field. *Matt Field on the Santa Fe Trail*. Collected by Clyde and Mae Reed Porter. Edited, with introduction and notes, by John E. Sunder.
30. James Knox Polk Miller. *The Road to Virginia City*: The Diary of James Knox Polk Miller. Edited by Andrew F. Rolle.
31. Benjamin Butler Harris. *The Gila Trail*: The Texas Argonauts and the California Gold Rush. Edited and annotated by Richard H. Dillon.
32. Lieutenant James H. Bradley. *The March of the Montana Column*: A Prelude to the Custer Disaster. Edited by Edgar I. Stewart. Out of print.
33. Heinrich Lienhard. *From St. Louis to Sutter's Fort, 1846*. Translated and edited by Erwin G. and Elisabeth K. Gudde.
34. Washington Irving. *The Adventures of Captain Bonneville, U.S.A., in the Rocky Mountains and the Far West*. Edited and introduction by Edgeley W. Todd.
35. Jean-Bernard Bossu. *Bossu's Travels in the Interior of North America, 1751–1762*. Translated and edited by Seymour Feiler.
36. Thomas D. Clark. *Travels in the New South*: A Bibliography. 2 vols.
37. John Lloyd Stephens. *Incidents of Travel in Yucatán*. With engravings by Frederick Catherwood. Edited and introduction by Victor Wolfgang von Hagen. 2 vols.
38. Richard A. Bartlett. *Great Surveys of the American West*.
39. Gloria Griffen Cline. *Exploring the Great Basin*. Out of print.
40. Francisco de Miranda. *The New Democracy in America*: Travels of Francisco de Miranda in the United States, 1783–84. Edited by John S. Ezell. Translated by Judson P. Wood.
41. Colonel Joseph K. F. Mansfield. *Mansfield on the Condition of the Western Forts, 1853–54*. Edited and introduction by Robert W. Frazer.
42. Louis Antoine de Bougainville. *Adventure in the Wilderness*: The American Journals of Louis Antoine de Bougainville, 1756–1760. Translated and edited by Edward P. Hamilton.

182